Daily
POWER
Thoughts

Daily POWER Thoughts

By Robert H. Schuller

Harvest House Publishers
Irvine, California 92714

Verses marked NASB are from the NEW AMERICAN STANDARD, copyright © The Lockman Foundation 1960, 1962, 1963, 1968, 1971, 1972, 1973, 1975 and are used by permission.

Verses marked RSV are from the REVISED STANDARD VERSION, copyright © 1946, 1952, 1971, 1973 and are used by permission.

Verses marked NIV are from THE NEW INTERNATIONAL VERSION, New Testament, Copyright © 1973 by New York International Bible Society and are used by permission.

Verses marked PHILLIPS are from the PHILLIPS NEW TESTAMENT, Copyright © J.B. Phillips, 1958, 1959, 1960, 1972 and are used by permission.

Verses marked KJV are from the KING JAMES VERSION.

All other verses are from THE LIVING BIBLE, Copyright © 1971, Tyndale House Publishers, Wheaton, Illinois. Used by permission.

DAILY POWER THOUGHTS

Copyright © Robert H. Schuller
Published by Harvest House Publishers
Library of Congress Catalog Card Number 77-68012
ISBN 0-89081-131-8 Cloth Gift Edition
ISBN 0-89081-123-7 Paper

Printed in the United States of America.

Presented To

_____

By _____

Date _____

Dedicated to

God's Possibility People
Everywhere

Introduction

In preparing this book, my dream is to help you enjoy the beautiful possibilities God has available for you.

A very important scripture in my life is Jeremiah 29:11: "For I know the plans I have for you . . . plans for good and not for evil, to give you a future and a hope" (TLB).

My prayer is that these *Daily Power Thoughts* will encourage you to discover and enjoy all of the Good and wonderful plans prepared for each of your todays.

As you read *Daily Power Thoughts*, be sure to put your reactions in writing on the response pages. I have found them to be most helpful to many people.

God loves you! Believe it and live in His love daily.

Robert Schuller

Robert Schuller
Garden Grove, California

CONTENTS

JULY

God Will!
Talking With God
Self-Love
Peak to Peek

AUGUST

Discover Yourself
It's Possible
The Future
God-Power Within
Enthusiasm For Today

SEPTEMBER

Never Be Afraid
Tranquilize Tension
Liberate Your Imagination
Winning Is Beginning

OCTOBER

Listen and Glisten
Exalt Courage
Scars Become Stars
Know Where You're Going

NOVEMBER

Grow Faith
Power Steering Living
Change!
Gratitude
Welcome the Unexpected

DECEMBER

Expect More
Expect Love
Expect Growth
Expect Miracles!

Think Possibilities

"I can never get away from my God! If I go up to heaven, you are there; if I go down to the place of the dead, you are there."

Psalm 139:7, 8

"I don't believe in God anymore. There is no God. I thought so once, but He left me and I am in hell now. There is no God!" The woman saying these words to me was in a mental hospital. I talked with her at length, but failed to help encourage her. I heard soon after that she had withdrawn and become silent.

Some months later, I returned to visit her again and found her completely transformed. What had happened? A young doctor walking through her ward had stopped to talk. "What's you name?" he asked. She didn't answer. "Well, my name is Dr. Heven," he said to her. Slowly her head raised. Her hollow eyes stared at the doctor. As he started to walk away, she touched his sleeve and asked him to repeat his name. "Dr. Heven," he said with a smile.

Into her mind leaked this tiny thought: "Dr. Heven. Heven. If Heven is here then this can't be hell. If Heven is here God must be here. God is here."

The next morning she walked down the corridor repeating out load a Bible verse she had learned as a child. For several days she did this and then gradually the healing power of God's word began to do its work. Her irrational association of heaven with Dr. Heven started to give way to rational thoughts. Soon—with a smile like a person slowly awakening from a deep and terrible nightmare— the power of God brought about a transformation in this woman's life and when I saw her last she was fully recovered and teaching school. God can work in our lives through the smallest trickle of hope that leaks into our mind!

Right where I am, God is present!

Think Possibilities

"For with God, nothing is impossible."

Matthew 17:20

Your days can be filled with happiness, thrilling excitement and youthful enthusiasm if you will learn to *think possibilities*. Most unhappiness and despair comes from problem thinking. When you focus on problems, you are defeated. But when your attention is on the possibilities that accompany any problem, you're on the road to success!

How do you think possibilities? Begin by deciding upon some big beautiful dream that seems impossible. Or you may want to identify some problem that is passing in on you now. Write down a description of your dream or

problem: _____

_____

_____

Now let your imagination run wild. Only your moral and ethical principles will limit you. Legal questions and money problems will not contstrict the flow of your creative ideas as you think of 10 ways to solve this problem or to bring your impossible dream into the realm of probability. Do it now!

1. _____   6. _____

2. _____   7. _____

3. _____   8. _____

4. _____   9. _____

5. _____   10. _____

> **I enter this day with high expectations and a happy heart for with God nothing is impossible!**

Think Possibilities

"All things are possible to him who believes!"
                                    Mark 9:23 NASB

When my wife and I came to California to build a great church, we were met on our arrival with the information that there were no available places to begin services. Nothing available! What ghastly, impossible, negative advice!

On our way to California, while driving in the car, my wife and I made a list of 10 possible places to meet. We were faced with a problem, and our list of 10 possible solutions became very valuable. My only other assets were a wife, a mortgaged organ and five hundred dollars.

I took the list and started checking out the possibilities. Number one on the list was a school. I quickly found out that the school boards in the area felt the law did not allow them to rent facilities to churches. So I went to my next option—a 7th-Day Adventist church. Since they meet on Saturday, why not rent their facilities on Sunday? But someone else had already thought of that and possibility number 2 was scratched off my list. Down the list I went— 3, 4, 5, 6, 7, 8. Everything was unavailable. Option number nine was a drive-in-theater. Three miles east of our home, I found the Orange Drive-In-Theater. The manager listened curiously put politely to my peculiar request. A week later he phoned and said, "It's yours to use on Sunday."

From that modest beginning, God has worked miracle after miracle. If you'll use your list, He'll do the same for you!

All things work together for good, because God works and I work!

Think Possibilities

"The things which are impossible with men are possible with God."

Luke 18:27KJV

This joy-producing, energy-generating, success-stimulating process will work miracles in your life if certain principles are followed. One of these basic principles is that your creative energies must be directed at a serious objective. There must be some deep inner concern which gets the creative energy started and keeps it going.

Only when your subconscious mind deeply believes the mind-bending project to be very, very important will the hidden powers slumbering deep in the dark regions of the unconscious rise up and awaken your creative conscious.

Some years ago I experienced an example of this potential principle. A group of us were sitting around discussing the serious illness of a mutual friend. This person's heart was failing fast and death was near. I recalled at the time the comment of a famous heart surgeon who said, "The invention of an artificial heart was impossible because it would require an unfailing, permanent power-generating source."

When I mentioned this, the group came up with several ideas. I remember one of these ideas clearly. The person suggested, "Why not keep the power source outside the chest cavity? Why not settle for temporary power sources and simply change batteries regularly?" Although we didn't know it at the time, we had just described the eventual solution to that "impossible" problem! If you care enough and "tune in" to God's ideas, your problem can be solved. Your dream can come true!

> I am confident because I have faith in God! I really believe He makes all things possible!

Think Possibilities

"You will keep on guiding me all my life with your wisdom and counsel."

Psalm 73:24

Once you have spotted what appears to be an opportunity, don't plunge recklessly ahead without asking sensible questions. Success-test your opportunities. Challenge all positive ideas by asking success-spotting questions. Let me give you my four success-spotting, possibility-measuring, opportunity-testing questions?

1. Will this project fill a vital human need? Is it practical and will it help people who are hurting? How does your project measure up? _____ _____

_____

2. Will this project inspire people? Other people are attracted to the individual or the project that inspires and uplifts the heart and the human spirit. Your project may help you most, but will your success inspire and uplift others? _____

_____

3. Can I do this project in an outstanding way? Excellence is a vital key to success. Can your project be both monumental and instrumental? _____

_____

4. Is your solution pace-setting? Almost anything that is being done can be done differently and better. And when God is involved in your project, it deserves to be pace-setting! How about your project? Is it pace-setting? _____

_____

**God is opening new ways to me.
My future is bright!**

Think Possibilities

"In this place I will give prosperity, says the Lord of hosts."

Haggai 2:9 RSV

If you commit yourself to a project—to a dream—you must assume that you will find solutions as you move along. To a degree there is a tinge of recklessness to being a possibility thinker. But confidently you assume that no one is a failure if he has tried to do something wonderful.

I have a close friend who is practicing possibility thinking in his business. If faced with a legal problem, then nothing short of changing the law will do. If a law is blocking progress, then that law must be changed.

This man decided to build a shopping center over a ten acre parcel of land through which a flood control channel flowed. One law prohibited construction over flood control channels. That law blocked the fulfillment of his dream of an elaborate and functional shopping center in an area that needed such a facility.

So there was only one thing to do. That law should be updated in accordance with modern construction possibilities. The result? He tried. He believed. He kept on pressing. He crusaded. And the law was changed! Today, the Brashears Center has a flood control channel flowing harmlessly inside a reinforced concrete tunnel underneath a twelve story building! Nothing is impossible to those who believe in God!

I abide in a constant flow of God's abundance circulating in and through my life and my plans! This is God's will for me!

Think Possibilities

*"What a glorious Lord! He who daily bears our burdens
also gives us our salvation."*

Psalm 68:19

Speaking at the University of the Pacific in Stockton,
California, I was impressed by the magnificent tower
which guards the entrance to this beautiful campus. The
tall Neo-Gothic structure rises stately and tall from a
spacious green-lawned island immediately within the
gates.

The University president told me how the tower was
built. Some years before, a water shortage developed and
engineers were called in to study the problem. They said,
"The only solution is a new water tower, and the only
place it can go is immediately inside the entrance of the
campus."

The thought of an ugly, monstrous water tank marring
the front entrance of the university was a nauseating
suggestion to the president. But on further thought, this
possibility-thinking man thought, "Perhaps this profane-
appearing structure could be made into a sublime
monument."

The result? The water tower was erected. Around it, 30
foot square cement was built rising 150 feet into the sky.
Stained-glass windows were placed on the top 50 feet of the
tower to hide the water tank. The lower two-thirds of the
tower were divided into nine floors and today houses
modern administration offices, a board room, and a radio
station. Few universities in the world have a more inspiring
architectural landmark to greet incoming students and
visitors. Proof-positive that every adversity hides a
possibility!

**I have the faith to believe that every
adversity hides a beautiful possibility!**

Live Possibilities

"I will keep on expecting you to help me. I praise you more and more."

Psalm 71:14

Possibility thinkers are resourceful people. They follow the old maxim: "Where there's a will, there's a way." One of my first experiences in Garden Grove was a meeting with six Protestant ministers. "How many homes are there in the city?" I asked. "Fourteen thousand," one minister answered. "Have you taken a census of the religious affiliation of these people?" I asked. Amused silence and negative nods gave me my answer.

"Let's get all the churces together and canvass all fourteen thousand homes," I enthused. "Then we'll find out who belongs to a church and we can work on those who don't."

Their response was not overly enthusiastic. "That's impossible," they countered. "Do you realize how long that would take?" And with that positive-idea-squelching question, they killed the idea.

I mentioned my disappointment to a businessman friend in my church, who was a *real* possibility thinker. "Fourteen thousand? That's easy!" he exclaimed. All we need is forty people who will agree to make three hundred fifty calls. My wife and I will make up sheets with thirty-five address on them. Then each person will take ten sheets and the job will be done!"

Great idea! He made up the sheets. We got the forty volunteers who came to a dinner on Friday and picked up their ten sheets. Two Saturdays later, fourteen thousand doorbells had been rung. Forty possibility thinkers did what six professionals insisted was impossible! There's a solution to every problem!

**God gives me a solution
to every problem!**

Live Possibilities

*"I will sing to the Lord because he has blessed me
so richly."*

Psalm 13:6

You must mentally picture success. You throw your
mind into the future. See your problem resolved. Imagine
your dream a reality! Listen to the sounds of success—
laughter, applause, congratulations! Enjoy, mentally, the
rich fruits of your accomplishment.

As you use your powers of fantasy to propel you into
the high feeling of proud achievement, enthusiasm begins
to bubble deep within you. Excitement enthralls you.
Energy surges within you as your desire mounts. With
God's help, you have conquered your objective! What a
great moment!

Picture again the problem or opportunity you wrote
down last week. Now picture what you will feel and what
the situation will be like when your objective is accomplished. Write down your imagined description or draw a
picture of the scene.

I am a beloved child of God. He sees me
with my needs and my opportunities and
He is at work with me in my task!

Live Possibilities

"This is the day the Lord has made. We will rejoice and be glad in it."

Psalm 118:24

Fred Hostrop is not only a confirmed possibility thinker, he lives and acts on his possibilities. He wrote to me recently, describing his condition:

"For years I have suffered from acromegaly, which is caused by a tumor on my pituitary gland. This makes my gland over-active, which in turn causes me to grow abnormally large. I'm 73 years old and still growing!

"My skeleton is four times larger than normal. I have severe backaches and headaches, as a result, almost constantly. I can't pick up anything on the floor or ground because I cannot bend over that far. Since my equilibrium is poor, I can't stand in any one place very long and I need two canes to help me walk. I can't walk more than 200 feet without collapsing.

"Dr. Schuller, the above description may sound like negative thinking. But instead of saying, 'I can't do this or that,' I think of the possibilities and say to myself, 'What *can* I do about this situation?'

"Here's an example of one thing I'm doing. I used to love to play golf, but I can't play on the golfcourse anymore. But I can enjoy playing in my own backyard." And with the letter he sent me a picture of one of his "Hostrop-inventions"—it picks up the golf ball and sets it on the tee. He adds, "Hurrah! I can even use this to pick up litter in our yard every day!"

Fred's faith in God and His possibilities have given him the courage to act upon his opportunities and not give up!

> **God is my help in every need!**

Live Possibilities

"So don't be afraid, little flock. For it gives your Father great happiness to give you the Kingdom."

Luke 12:32

The great violinist Paganini was once performing before a most distinguished audience. Suddenly, one of the strings on his violin snapped. The audience gasped, but the master musician continued unruffled to play on the three remaining strings.

Snap!—a second string broke. Still Paganini played on without hesitation. Then, with a sharp crack, a third string broke! The audience now became awestruck. For a brief moment, the artist stopped, raised his famous Stradivarius violin high with one hand and announced, "One string— and Paganini."

With furious skill and the matchless discipline of a gifted craftsman, he finished the selection on a single string. The performance was done with such matchless perfection, the audience rose together and gave him a tumultuous ovation.

There will be times in your life that one string after another will snap. You will go through circumstances that would make quitters out of lesser men or women. You need to insure yourself against "drop-out-itis." You do this by connecting yourself with an unfailing spiritual power source.

You will not quit. You will keep up your brave performance because the very power of the Eternal God surges deep within your being!

I let the power of God flow through me. He strengthens me and gives me the desire to get started and keep going!

Live Possibilities

"But I was trusting you, O Lord. I said, 'You alone are my God; my times are in your hands. Rescue me from those who hunt me down relentlessly.'"

Psalm 31:14, 15

No force or emotion is more paralyzing than fear. One of two emotions will dominate and drive you—either faith or fear. Like oil and water, the two do not mix. The only antidote to fear is faith!

When it comes to you living your possibilities, what fears attack you? Fear of failure? Fear of embarrassment? Stop now and identify the negative fears that threaten to paralyze you:

1. _____

2. _____

3. _____

Now put your faith to work and write to God, in the form of a prayer, and give him these fears. Affirm your faith in His power at work in your life:

Dear God, _____

_____

_____

_____ *Amen!*

**My fears are gone!
My faith is growing stronger!**

Live Possibilities

*"For God alone my soul waits in silence, for my hope is
from him."*

Psalm 62:5 RSV

Modern chemistry is able to turn almost any cast-off
product into a useful and profitable enterprise. Can you
find something that is being discarded as worthless
material?

An accountant at a Midwestern meat-packing plant said,
"The only part of the hog we throw away is the squeal." A
swampy area in Southern California was considered
worthless until an enterprising developer imagined
channels dug to turn the swamp into a beautiful lake, with
canals leading off from the lake like spokes from the hub of
a wheel. He imagined houses built on the canals with a pri-
vate dock for each owner. He has made millions on
this idea.

There was a gypsum mine near Grand Rapids,
Michigan, which opened in 1907. It was a multi-million
dollar plant until 1943, when it was considered, "finished."
An imaginative opportunity-spotting possibility thinker
saw potential in that mine. The underground tunnels had a
constant temperature of fifty degrees. That old gypsum
mine is today a very profitable storage company. Turkeys,
eggs, nuts, potatoes, and beef are just a few of the many
foodstuffs stored underground.

Simon was a vacillating fisherman with good intentions,
but no backbone. Jesus saw within him the possibilities of
leadership. He gave Simon a new name—Peter—and a new
responsibility as leader in the first church.

When God looks at you, what great possibilities does
He see?

As a child of God I can expect
to meet today with confidence!

Live Possibilities

Turn, O Lord, my fears around.
Let them become a positive force
for good in my life until I—
Fear not that I might fail.
  But fear rather that I might never dare to discover my
  potential.
Fear not that I might be hurt.
  But fear rather that I might never experience growing
  pains.
Fear not that I might love and lose.
  But fear rather that I might never love at all.
Fear not that people may laugh at my mistakes.
  But fear rather that God will say to me "O ye of little
  faith."
Fear not that I might fail if try again.
  But fear rather that I might miss my greatest chance for
  happiness if I failed to give hope another opportunity.
Amen.

Commit Yourself!

"Love surrounds those who trust in the Lord. So rejoice in Him and shout for joy!"

Psalm 32:10, 11

Some time ago, Mrs. Schuller and I joined with over a thousand friends—including many of Hollywood's great stars—to salute Ethel Waters. It was a beautiful evening! But the greatest part of the event was when Ethel Waters herself, in her own inimitable, open, honest and transparent style, told the people gathered how happy she was because Jesus was in her heart.

We all sat enthralled as Ethel performed again, and as we had the privilege of seeing film playbacks of her great life, as she sang and talked as only Ethel Waters can, I thought again of the tremendous odds she had overcome.

She was born an illegitimate child and raised in poverty in the ghetto. By every standard of modern psychology, Ethel should have been an emotionally deprived and emotionally scarred person with a very limited range of emotional development.

But when you see and hear her, you find one of the greatest, biggest, most beautiful souls that walks on planet earth! And there is no way to explain her life except that something gave her a great big, loving, bubbling, beautiful heart. She says that that something is a somebody— His name is Jesus!

I am enriched and filled to bubbling over—flowing by the power of my indwelling Lord!

Commit Yourself!

"There are three things that remain—faith, hope and love—and the greatest of these is love."

1 Corinthians 13:13

Over the years I have been working on a list of what I call the seven positive human values. My list started while attending a World Psychiatric Congress. The subject for the last session was "Human Values in Psychotherapy." The program did not say what these values were, so in anticipation of that seminar, I made my own list.

When that final event of the Congress finally arrived, I was ready. The first speaker, an American, delivered a lecture on the importance of *faith* in the human life. He was followed by a West German, who dramatically portrayed the dynamic value of *hope*. He described the sudden change that occurs when something ignites the spark of hope within a person—healing takes place and life returns.

The final lecturer, from Peru, presented a paper on the importance of *love*. As I left the lecture hall, I was amazed at how close the conclusions of these three psychiatrists were to the Bible. Their list was the same as St. Paul's.

What dynamic human values would you add to that list? Think a moment and then write down any additional values which you feel are important:

_____

_____

_____

> **My heart is tuned to the spirit of God.
> I can feel His values becoming
> my values!**

Commit Yourself!

"Commit everything you do to the Lord. Trust him to help you do it and he will.

Psalm 37:5

The first value on my list is COMMITMENT—that is my word for faith. I've deliberately chosen not to use the word faith, because for too many people, this word is a "cop-out." It is simply too easy to say—"Oh, I believe," or "Yes, I think God can do it." Anyone can say those words. That's faith, but on a very shallow level. And a shallow faith does not help when the going gets rough!

So I use the word COMMITMENT. That is FAITH IN ACTION! Commitment is putting your faith on the line. It is coming clean; being honest and forthright; taking action!

As a human being, you have three powers which animals do not have. You have the power to choose—to make a vocal choice. You have the power to react in an intelligent, rational and logical way. And third, you have the power to make commitments!

Oscar Wilde once said, "An idea that isn't risky is hardly worth calling an idea." Make your commitment! Strong strength comes to provide you with support and energy. Enormous spiritual forces are unleashed as you commit yourself in action to Jesus Christ.

I rejoice in the vibrant, God-given power within me as I commit myself to action!

Commit Yourself!

"Commit your work to the Lord, then it will succeed."
                                        Proverbs 16:3

A major source of personal fatigue and lack of human energy, excitement and enthusiasm is caused by the lack of commitment.

But when you make that COMMITMENT, guess what happens? Enormous power flows into your mind—brilliant flashes of insight explode within you! The energy to say "no" to what is wrong and "yes" to what is right surges within. And it is amazing what you will be able to do. All because you make a commitment.

Where is your faith undecisive? What commitments are you attempting to ignore? Make your commitment to action now! Then write it down!

MY COMMITMENT

_____

_____

_____

_____

_____

_____

I can feel the power of Christ within me
at work as I commit myself to Him
and to a plan of action!

Commit Yourself!

"If you wait for perfect conditions, you will never get anything done."

Ecclesiastes 11:4

The New American Standard Bible translates our verse this way, "He who watches the wind will not sow and he who looks at the clouds will not reap."

Now, being born on an Iowa farm, I know what that means. If the farmer thinks a wind is going to come up, he puts off sowing his seeds. For if you try to sow in the wind, the gusts will only blow the seed away before it can penetrate the ground and be fertilized. But you might never plant your crop if you are too cautious.

On the other hand when the wheat or oats become ripe, and if the farmer thinks it might rain, he will put off cutting the wheat or oats, because if the grain gets soggy with rain right after it is cut, it is ruined. The soggy grain gets moldy and never dries out. But if you never reap your harvest, the grain will rot anyway!

If you feel a breeze coming up, you'll never sow your seed. Or if you see some clouds, you'll never reap. And you'll never get started! Now that's the word of God! COMMITMENT is making an all-out plunge of faith before you can be sure how anything is going to turn out. The most important commitment you can make is to Jesus Christ. That is where you need to begin! Do it now!

Today, Lord I am not going to look at conditions. Instead, I am looking at You and draw from You the power to begin!

Commit Yourself!

"See, the Lord is for me!"

Isaiah 50:9

Before we built our present sanctuary, this area was nothing but orange groves with some walnut trees. One day I parked my car at the edge of the field to pray. Suddenly I heard the snap of a twig. I looked up and saw a man coming at me with a shotgun. I appeared startled, but he smiled and said, "I'm sorry, I didn't mean to frighten you."

With a heavy accent, he continued, "I just came to America from Europe. We are very poor so I hunt rabbits for our food, but I haven't seen any today."

"Look," I enthused," over there. There's some rabbits."

"Oh," he responded dejectedly, "they are too far away. I could never get them."

"Why don't you sneak up on them?" I suggested.

Then he went into an explanation about the way a rabbit feels vibrations through the bottom of his feet. He was a real impossibility thinker! But I guess his empty stomach helped me convince him to try and sneak up on them. "Maybe I'll try," he finally agreed.

Ever so slowly he started sneaking up on the rabbits. I kept thinking he was close enough, but still he crept along. Finally he raised his gun and fired! He took off running into the grove and a minute later reappeared with his rabbit—dinner for his family.

"Maybe I'll try," he said. And that commitment meant his family had dinner that night!

> **Lord, I am going to try beginning today!**

Commit Yourself!

"Because the Lord helps me, I will not be dismayed; there-fore I have set my face like flint to do his will, and I know that I will triumph."

Isaiah 50:7

Two of the greatest people I've ever known were Dorothy and Henry Poppen. They served over 40 years in China, preaching, teaching, and building schools, hospitals, and churches.

Those were dangerous years. Besides the risk of disease, bandits, plague and accidents at sea or in the mountains, they were driven out of China by the Communists, barely escaping with their lives.

One day I asked Dorothy, "What drove you onward all those years?"

"We thrive on adventure!" she answered with fire in her eyes.

That dynamic adventure-tension in both Henry and Dorothy was baptized by the Spirit of Jesus Christ and grew out of a commitment they made early in life. What a way to live!

How are you doing on your commitment project? If you find yourself wavering or doubting, simply reaffirm your commitment. And then live expectantly the life full of adventure.

COMMITMENT—The first of seven life-changing human values—is where living really begins!

With every breath I breathe, I recommit myself to all of God's great possibilities for me today!

Be Confident!

O God,

I come to you to find power
    to be really strong.
Save me from the make-believe strengths
    that leave me weak.
Help me be the kind of person
    nothing can upset,
    for I am confident within!
I expose myself to your strength.

I believe you are taking away from me
    all negative thinking.
    all inclination to shun responsibility,
    all fearful attitudes.
You are inspiring me now to face life
    with confidence
    and with a song!
           Thank you Lord.
           Amen.

Be Confident!

*"Expect God to act! For I know that I shall again have
plenty of reasons to praise him for all that he will do. He is
my help! He is my God!"*

Psalm 42:11

COMMITMENT—faith in action—is the first human
value on my list. If you make a commitment, then you
must have CONFIDENCE. You must believe that you can,
with God's help, accomplish the task to which you have
commited yourself.

Now self-confidence is just like the manna that fell from
heaven to feed the Israelites in the wilderness. It doesn't
last very long unless you are constantly working at
renewing your sense of confidence.

What are you doing this week that helps you feel more
confident? _____

_____

What other things do you enjoy that helps you feel good
about yourself? _____

_____

Continue now, to think of other ways that you can build
a positive, self-affirming, growth-producing feeling of
self-confidence.

Thank you, God, for all the good
reasons you give me for feeling good
about myself. Thanks for loving me!

Be Confident!

"So there is now no condemnation awaiting those who belong to Christ Jesus."

Romans 8:1

Nothing is more important than your own self-confidence and your own affirmative self-image. That's why the second dynamic human value on my list is CONFIDENCE.

I heard the story of a minister who was very depressed and had a very negative self-image. He was the senior minister and things obviously were not going right.

Feeling very low, he entered the sanctuary, knelt at the altar and prayed a very negative prayer. "O God, I am nothing. I am nothing," he repeated over and over again.

Just at that point, the assistant minister walked by and was very impressed by the senior minister's humility. So he joined him in praying, "O Lord, I am nothing. I, too, am nothing."

At that moment the janitor happened to enter the auditorium and was awestruck by the humility of the leaders of the church. Not to be outdone, he joined them at the altar and said, "O Lord, I, too, am nothing, nothing, nothing."

The assistant minister stopped, looked at the janitor, then turned to the senior pastor and said, "Now look who thinks he's nothing."

I chuckle everytime I think of that story, but I also feel like crying because so many Christians believe in that kind of humility. That concept is not Christian humility! God wants you to be confident for you are made in His image!

> O God, I am great! I am great because You made me in Your image! Wow! I am made in God's image!

Be Confident!

"For I know the one in whom I trust, and I am sure that he is able to safely guard all that I have given him until the day of his return."

2 Timothy 1:12

The story of Zacchaeus is a remarkable one. Jesus was passing through Jericho one day surrounded by people trying to get a glimpse of the Miracle Worker! One man who was too short to see over the crowds, ran ahead and climbed into a sycamore tree beside the road. He clung to the strong branches of that enormous tree and watched for Jesus.

Zacchaeus was one of the most influential Jews in the Roman tax-collecting business. But he was a traitor to his own people—a Jew who surrendered his patriotism by selling out to the Romans!

The small man forfeited his patriotism to get money. He thought money would give him power and power would give him self-confidence!

Now why would Zacchaeus want to see Jesus? To collect money? No! Zacchaeus was searching for self-confidence, which is really a hunger for God. Only God can satisfy. Money, power, following the crowd—none of these provide the deep satisfaction that comes when we place ourselves in a position to find God. That's why Zacchaeus climbed the tree! He put himself in a place where he and God could meet!

I live today with faith and confidence,
for God knows me and is with me.
I cannot fail!

Be Confident!

"He will hold you aloft in his hands for all to see—a
splendid crown for the King of kings."

Isaiah 62:3

Imagine that you and a friend are walking along a dusty road outside of Jerusalem, around the year 31 A.D. As you walk, someone approaches from the other direction—a man. Your friend knows the man, and stops to introduce you to him. He says, "Jesus, I want you to meet (your name)."

What would you like your friend to tell Jesus about you?

Write out your introduction and then read it over several times during the next few days: _____

_____

_____

_____

_____

_____

_____

_____

> Everyday, I feel more confident because I am a child of God. I am confident today so I am going to tackle that impossible task I have been putting off.

Be Confident!

"How precious it is, Lord, to realize that you are thinking about me constantly!

Psalm 139:17

Imagine how Zacchaeus must have felt when Jesus called him by name. Jesus knew Zacchaeus even before they met! There was Zacchaeus, inwardly all torn up by guilt. He probably expected a sermon, a tirade, a scolding or a slap on the wrist from Jesus. Instead, Jesus looked at him and said, "Zacchaeus, I am going to be a guest in your home today!"

Go back to the scene you imagined yesterday. Your friend has just introduced Jesus to you, and told Him several things about you. Now Jesus speaks and says, "It's good to meet you, but I already know you. I know that you . . .

Now write down what Jesus would say about you:

_____

_____

_____

_____

_____

_____

> Jesus loves me and accepts me as I am.
> If I am loved and accepted by the
> Creator of the universe, then I can
> love and accept myself today!

Be Confident!

"If God is on our side, who can ever be against us?"
Romans 8:31

I have *confidence!* Let me tell you where I get it: God is my Father! Jesus Christ is my personal Savior! The Holy Spirit lives in me!

God has reached down and of all these billions of human beings, He has spotted you, called you by name, lifted you up and embraced you. He has forgiven you of your sins, put His arms around you and said, "Look, we're going to walk through life together, you and I!" Wow!

There is nothing greater than that. It's called salvation. When you are born again, you discover the source of *confidence!*

Once there was a rabbi who was asked, "When should a man repent?" And the wise old rabbi who answered, "On the last day of his life."

"But," they said, "none of us can be sure which day is the last day of our life."

The rabbi smiled and said, "Then repent now." Repentance is not a negative self-condemnation. Repentance is "turning around" to walk God's way!

Have you experienced salvation? Someday you and I will stand before God, and He wants to compliment and praise us. Decide today to invite Jesus Christ to live within you. Discover the source of real self-confidence! After all, if God is on your side everybody else might as well be also.

> I invite You into my life, Lord Jesus.
> Thank you for seeing the possibilities
> within me, for not condemning me,
> and for being for me!

Persevere!

"I have prayed for you that your faith may not fail."
Luke 22:31 RSV

What's the best thing that has happened to you in the past five years? _____

_____

_____

_____

If you had a difficult time thinking of any "best" thing, it's probably your fault. Because, you see, God has given you great possibilities! And the secret of dynamic and effective living is really up to you.

Making confident commitments unlocks the door, which means that you establish a long-range goal and objective. Too many people have only a vague idea of what they want to accomplish in their own lifetime. Therefore nothing of any significance ever happens.

To live an exciting, growing life, you first establish a firm objective to which you can confidently commit yourself. Then translate this objective into immediate steps, intermediate steps, long-range steps and ultimate steps.

Once you've done this, all you need is our third dynamic human value—PERSEVERANCE! PERSEVERANCE makes it possible for you to live in such a spirit that good things *will* happen to you!

I am filled with the joyous, triumphant, overcoming and persevering spirit of Jesus Christ!

Persevere!

"Be strong with the strength Christ Jesus gives you."
2 Timothy 2:1

Let's try working on a goal. Describe one important objective to which you would like to be confidently committed: _____

_____

Now describe two or more mere long-range steps that would have to be taken in order for you to reach your objective:

1. _____

2. _____

Good! Now take one of the above steps, and outline all of the immediate and intermediate measures that you will need to accomplish in order to reach your long-range step in the direction of your goal. (You will probably want to expand all of this on a separate sheet of paper.)

1. _____

2. _____

3. _____

You will find it helpful to estimate the amount of time it will take to meet your immediate and intermediate objectives, but do not be afraid to change the dates if you find it is taking longer than you planned.

> I am strong in the Lord. I can keep on keeping on until my goals are reached. Thank you, Lord!

Persevere!

"The Lord will work out his plans for my life—for you lovingkindness, Lord, continues forever."

Psalm 138:8

A Sunday School class was discussing the story of Jonah. The teacher explained how the Lord punished Jonah for running away from Him by arranging for a huge fish to swallow the frightened man. For three days Jonah cried out to the Lord praising and thanking Him from the belly of that great fish. On the third day God ordered the fish to spit Jonah onto the beach.

In closing, the teacher asked her students, "What does this story teach us?"

One little boy quickly answered, "Well, I think the story teaches us that you can't keep a good man down!"

He was right you know! And that's why *perseverance* is on my list of dynamic, life-changing values. But we all have experiences at times in our life when we are really down. Perhaps there is something happening to you this week that threatens to hold you back or knock you down. Describe the situation: _____

_____

_____

Now, like Jonah prayed inside the whale, confidently commit this situation to God in prayer. When Jonah had lost all hope, he turned his thoughts once more to the Lord. His reason? "For my deliverance comes from the Lord alone."

> I can feel the barriers falling down.
> What has appeared to me to be an
> impossible situation is fast becoming
> a possibility!

Persevere!

"But grow in spiritual strength and become better acquainted with our Lord and Savior Jesus Christ."
                                            2 Peter 3:18

I read the other day about a professional athlete who, the newspaper says, is still holding out. They do not think he will sign his contract until he gets anything he wants. But, the article continued, he is in danger of holding out too long. He may not only end up without what he wants, he may also end up without a contract.

Some people are hold-outs in life. They will hold out until they can be sure they will succeed. They will hold out until there are no uncertain ties or until they can see a solution to every problem. They want to wait until there are no risks. They forget that holding out on life can be the biggest risk of all.

"THE SADDEST WORDS OF
TONGUE OR PEN ARE THESE:

'IT MIGHT HAVE BEEN!' "

"Will it work out?" "Can I be sure?" "Can I wait until the risk is gone?" These negative thoughts come like birds snapping up the seed of positive, life-renewing, growth-producing, risk-taking thoughts that are intended to inspire us to live happier, more joy filled lives. Determine today to stop holding out. Sign the contract. Take the risk.

I am living today controlled by my
God-inspired positive ideas!

Persevere!

"Since future victory is sure, be strong and steady, always abounding in the Lord's work, for you know that nothing you do for the Lord is ever wasted."

1 Corinthians 15:58

A woman went on a shopping spree and came home with a beautiful but expensive dress! Cautiously, she showed the lavish purchase to her husband. But when he heard the price, he threw up his hands in horror and asked, "How could you do it?"

"The devil made me do it," she answered.

"But," her husband continued, "why didn't you do like it tells you in the Bible and say, 'Get thee behind me, Satan?' "

"I did," she coyle replied, "and I heard him say to me, 'It looks beautiful from behind, dear.' "

The cleverest thing about the devil is that he makes us think that HE did it. And that tricky twist of words takes you and me off the hook. If we can blame the devil—or anything or anyone else—we are not responsible for our own behavior! And then it is not our fault if we sin or if we fail.

Now we can be sure that the devil does not want us to succeed. He will try to block us with negative thoughts and negative people. But know this for certain: "Christ has made us free!" (Galatians 5:1). When we belong to Jesus Christ, we belong to the one who has already defeated the devil. And we are free to enjoy all of God's great possibilities for our lives!

> **I can meet today with strength and perseverance, for my battles have already been won by Christ Jesus!**

Persevere!

POSSBILITY THINKERS CREED

When faced
With a mountain
I WILL NOT QUIT! .
I Will keep on striving until
I climb over, find a pass through,
tunnel underneath—or simply
stay and turn the mountain
into a gold mine
with God's help!

Persevere!

"When a person falls, he jumps up again!"

Jeremiah 8:4

A stock broker I know recently went through a very difficult time in his business. He lost almost everything he owned. During this time he decided to practice possibility thinking and believed that God could help him.

The first thing he decided was that he had to find a way to feed his family. He had no money, but he took his station wagon out at four o'clock in the morning and drove down the alleys of his neighborhood picking up all the old newspapers he could find in people's trash. In the evening when no one could recognize him, he did the same thing. That first week he earned almost $70.00 collecting old papers and selling them.

Then he got his boys into the act. They went to apartment houses and offered to collect old newspapers. The managers of the apartment house thought it was a great way to be rid of some trash. When he told me this story, he was making over $1000 a month collecting old newspapers, while still working at his brokerage office.

His associates can't understand why he is so happy. He tells them, "I practice possibility thinking and I have faith in God." And I could add to that the fact that he had developed the dynamic human value of PERSEVERANCE!

I rejoice in my developing ability to persevere. God and I are up to doing some great things today!

Have Courage!

"Be strong! Be courageous! Do not be afraid . . . For the Lord your God will be with you. He will neither fail you nor forsake you."

Deuteronomy 31:6

Dr. Henry Poppen, one of the first missionaries to go to China, and who spent over forty years there, once told me about the time he went to a remote village where presumably missonaries had never before visited.

Dr. Poppen told them about Jesus—how He was gentle, kind, loving and able to forgive easily. When he finished talking about Jesus, one of the village men came to him and said, "Oh, we know Jesus! He has been here!"

"No, no," the missionary protested, "Jesus lived and died in a country far from here long ago."

"Oh no," the people replied. "He died here. Come, we'll show you his grave."

The villagers led Dr. Poppen outside the city to a Chinese cemetery where an American was buried. There on the tombstone was the name of a Christian medical doctor who, all on his own, felt called by God to go and live in this village, and to die there. When the villagers heard what Jesus was like, they remembered the doctor.

COURAGE—the fourth dynamic human value on my list. And how courageous that doctor must have been. He knew what St. Paul meant when he wrote, "We, too, are weak in our bodies . . . but now we live and are strong . . . and have all of God's power to use!" (2 Corinthians 13:4).

> **By the power of Christ in me,
> I am courageous!**

Have Courage!

"Wait for the Lord, and he will come and save you! Be brave, stouthearted and courageous."

Psalm 27:14

A missionary in India told how he was kneeling at his bed praying one night when a giant python snake uncoiled itself from the rafters and wrapped itself around his body.

The python, which is not uncommon to that area of India, kills its victim by squeezing it to death. The missionary told how a bible verse immediately came to mind as the meandering serpent enveloped his body. *"In quietness and confidence is your strength"* (Isaiah 30:15) And suddenly he was filled with the calm assurance that God was in control! He remained perfectly still, praying and meditating like he never had before!

Had he struggled, hesitated or tensed up, the coils of the mighty creature would have constricted and crushed him! Instead he waited, prayed, stayed calm and didn't move a muscle. Slowly, the snake uncoiled itself and retreated back to the rafters.

Most of us admire that kind of quiet COURAGE. I don't believe there is a value that is more recognizable and admirable in a human life than courage. Claim the courage that is yours as a child of God. God wants you to be courageous!

I am made for confident, courageous living. Today I am living courageously. I can feel my fears slipping away as God fills me with courage!

Have Courage!

"Be strong, be brave, and do not be afraid . . . for we have the Lord our God to fight our battles for us!"
2 Chronicles 32:7, 8

This week we have seen two examples of COURAGE, both different. One lived boldly and courageously. The other had the courage to be still and therefore lived. Perhaps you feel a strong desire for more courage in your own life. Take a moment and reflect on your circumstances. Where in your life could you be more courageous?

_____

_____

_____

Now describe how you would feel and act if you had more courage: _____

_____

_____

_____

_____

I want to challenge you to live today believing that what you have just written is true! And if you believe it, you will discover that it is true!

> **This remarkable spirit of courage is overpowering me. What a relief!**

Have Courage!

"The Lord is my helper and I am not afraid of anything that mere man can do to me."

Hebrews 13:6

Some years ago a nameless person went to an orphanage and asked, "Is there any orphan here that nobody wants?" The matron answered, "Indeed there is. She's ten years old, ugly to look at and has a very horrible hunchback. In fact, the only decent thing about her is her name—Mercy Goodfaith."

The inquirer said, "That's exactly the child I want." And together they left.

Thirty-five years later, the head of the Orphanage Inspection Department in the state of Iowa turned in a report about another orphanage that said, "This home is outstanding. It is clean, the food is good, and the matron of the place has a soul that oozes love.

"All of the children are well-cared for and show the effects of the matron's love. As they gathered at the piano following dinner, I observed an atmosphere unlike any I have seen in my work. Never have I seen such beautiful eyes as in that matron. They were so stunning that I almost forgot how homely her face was and how unattractive was the hunchback. Her name is Mercy Goodfaith."

Because some nameless person had the courage to care for an ugly orphan, Mercy Goodfaith learned how to love and has multiplied that love a hundred times over. My prayer for you today is that God will give you the COURAGE to care!

> I dare to believe that God is giving me the courage to care enough to do something wonderful today!

Have Courage!

"Share each other's troubles and problems, and so obey our Lord's command."

Galatians 6:2

Sometimes God sends into our lives people who are unlovely and it is very difficult to care for them. And all too often, these people give us plenty of reasons for not caring, when in reality they need to be cared for.

What unlovely, uncaring person has God sent into your life recently? Describe why it is hard for you to be caring to this person:

1. _____

2. _____

3. _____

4. _____

5. _____

6. _____

7. _____

Inch by inch, I can feel my love for_____growing! I have the courage to care!

Have Courage!

"Out of his glorious, unlimited resources he will give you the mighty inner strengthening of his Holy Spirit."

Ephesians 3:16

For over fifteen years, Lois had cancer. Yet all of those years she served as my personal secretary. I never in my life expect to meet anyone more courageous than she was.

Often she had days when she was so ill that getting out of bed took all the strength she had! Lois would deliberately fall out of bed, walk on hands and knees to the bathroom, reach for the sink and pull herself up. Finally standing on her feet, she would pull a brush through her hair, wash, and then force herself to get dressed.

Then she would stumble into the kitchen, drink some water, eat a dry piece of toast, search for her purse and walk to the door. Perspiration pouring off her forehead, she would pull herself up, look at her husband and say, "Well, Ralph, I think I can make it now."

And she would walk out the door, get into her car and drive to the church. She was always there before me, and when I came in with my usual greeting: "Good morning, how are you?" she would smile and say, "Great!" And I never knew until after her funeral what she went through those fifteen years. Her courage kept her alive and caring through those years. Only God can give you that kind of COURAGE!

> Come, Lord, and transform my melancholy spirit until my heart erupts in joy and courageous happiness!

Peace Be Yours

"In quietness and confidence is your strength."
                                              Isaiah 30:15

I watched my youngest daughter struggle over her spelling the other night. I remembered how I would write the words over ten times, and then if I missed one on the test, the teacher made us write them twenty-five times! Then I thought, "What if I wrote an affirmation ten times?" And I tried it. It was amazing! By the third time, the words began to take on a new clarity. By the tenth writing, I had added some thoughts and the affirmation was *mine*.

Try it yourself. Take the verse from Isaiah 30:15 and change it to read, *"In quietness and confidence is my strength."* Slowly and thoughtfully write it out eight times.

1. _____

2. _____

3. _____

4. _____

5. _____

6. _____

7. _____

8. _____

In quietness and confidence is my strength and courage for living today!

Peace Be Yours

*"I am leaving you with a gift—peace of mind and heart!
And the peace I give isn't fragile like the peace the world
gives."*

John 14:27

There was a Jewish lad who, as a young boy, decided to
make a list of the great values he would pursue in his lifetime. He wrote down fame, thought awhile, and then
added fortune to his list. Sometime later he added good
health to the other two goals he had chosen. When he was
satisfied that his list was complete, he presented his list to
his rabbi, who scanned it quickly.

The rabbi shook his head and said, "No, no. You have
missed one of the most important values of life, and that is
peace of mind. What good is money, what good is fame,
what good is a fortune or good health if you do not have
PEACE at the core of your life?"

The Jewish people today still have this same greeting.
"Shalom"—meaning PEACE. It was customary in the time
Jesus lived to greet each other with that wonderful word.

It was very natural then for Jesus to utter these words
just hours before He died on the cross:

*"I am leaving you with a gift—peace of mind and
Heart! And the peace I give you isn't fragile like
the peace the world gives. So don't be troubled or
afraid." [John 14:27].*

These words are for you today! And that is why PEACE
is on my list of dynamic human values.

> **The peace of God rules my heart today.
> Nothing can disturb the calm peace
> of my soul!**

Peace Be Yours

*"I have told you all this so that you will have peace of heart
and mind. Here on earth you will have many trials and
sorrows; but cheer up, for I have overcome the world."*
                                        John 16:33

How would you define the word PEACE? Some definitions would include the idea of "the absence of war and
conflict." Other definitions might simply say, "no hassles."
Yet, when I read Jesus' words about peace in the midst of
trials and sorrows, I question these definitions.

How about your definition—how would you describe
the meaning of PEACE? Write out a definition or simply
list the qualities or characteristics of the meaning of peace:

_____

_____

_____

_____

_____

_____

_____

_____

> **At the center of the great storm of
> activity that surrounds my life, I feel
> peaceful deep within my being!**

Peace Be Yours

"He will keep in perfect peace all those who trust in him, whose thoughts turn often to the Lord."

Isaiah 26:3

I discovered the secret to peace of mind some years ago as I was returning from a special mission in Korea. On the way home, I stopped in Hawaii and there I saw a beautiful sculptured statue of Jesus Christ returning to the sheepfold carrying the lamb that had been lost.

Jesus' weary expression confirmed my belief that He had spent long hours walking up and down the steep slopes, through crevices and canyons, until He finally found the lost sheep.

What struck me particularly about the statue was the peaceful appearance of the lamb as it seemed to curl itself around the neck of the Good Shepherd. The two front feet of the little sheep were folded gently, the one relaxed across the other. You could almost sense the feeling that perhaps the baby lamb was still trembling a little and his tiny body was still damp and cold. But as he relaxed on the shoulder of Jesus, he was warming up and a sense of calmness and security swept over him.

He was safe on the shoulder of the Good Shepherd. He was lost, but now he'd been found. What peace flooded his being as the lost sheep returned to the fold. He had been saved!

The secret of real peace of mind is to be found in Jesus; born anew through His Spirit, and trusting your future to Him! Jesus Christ is the source of true PEACE.

As I turn my attention to Jesus my Savior, I can feel tension and anxiety slipping away and a strong awareness of peace floods my being!

Peace Be Yours

"Let the peace of heart which comes from Christ be always present in your heart and lives, for this is your responsibility and privilege as members of his body."

Colossians 3:15

Peace of heart and mind—your privilege and responsibility! Take a moment now and meditate and pray. Ask God to make you aware of the areas in your life where you are not experiencing peace. What is spoiling your peace of mind? After praying and meditating, write down the areas that God brings to your attention: _____

_____

_____

_____

_____

When you finish your list, take each item and turn the source of unpeacefulness back to God. He has promised you that peace of heart and mind is your privilege. Trust Him to keep His promise to you!

Now write out an affirming prayer of thankfulness for the sense of PEACE that God is now giving you:

_____

_____

> God's peace is mine today. I will allow nothing to rob me of God's gift of peace of heart and mind!

Peace Be Yours

"May peace and blessing be yours from God the Father and from the Lord Jesus Christ."

Galatians 1:3

A man lived in the mountains with his little daughter. They raised sheep. One day they went out looking for a missing lamb and found the small animal caught in a thorny thicket. Carefully, and ever so gently they lifted the lamb out, but it was still scratched and bleeding in places. The little girl was crying as she said, "Father, that's a bad tree. Let's cut it down."

The next day they returned with an ax to cut the tree down. As they approached the thorny branches, the little girl saw a small bird flutter down to a branch, open its beak and grab a mouthful of wool that had been left on a thorn as the little lamb had struggled the day before. The tiny bird tugged and tugged and tugged until he had a mouthful of wool and then he flew away.

The little girl looked up at her father and said, "I think God has a good reason for this thorny tree. I don't think we should cut it down for the thorns are helping that bird get soft wool for its baby's nest."

Don't allow the thorns of life to mar your perspective. The thorns may hurt and cut and seem to have no purpose. But in God's great plan and purpose for you, every thorn can be an opportunity for increasing your vision of God's great possibility in your life. When your path is thorny, be at PEACE, for God is walking with you!

I am resting in God's peace today. His peace is more overwhelming than any of life's circumstances.

Peace Be Yours

"When he giveth quietness, who then can make trouble?
And when he hideth his face, who then can behold him?
Whether it be done against a nation, or against a man
only."

Job 34:29 KJV

"I will lie down in peace and sleep, for though I am alone,
O Lord, you will keep me safe."

Psalm 4:8

"He will give his people strength. He will bless them with
peace."

Psalm 29:11

". . . heaven's dawn is about to break upon us, to give light
to those who sit in darkness and death's shadow, and to
guide us to the path of peace."

Luke 1:78-79

"May the Lord of peace himself give you his peace no
matter what happens. The Lord be with you all."

2 Thessalonians 3:16

". . . for the good man—the blameless, the upright, the
man of peace—he has a wonderful future ahead of him.
For him there is a happy ending."

Psalm 37:37

Peace Be Yours

"Therefore being justified by faith we have peace with God through our Lord Jesus Christ."

Romans 5:1 KJV

Henry Drummonds tells the story of two artists who were commissioned to paint a picture that would depict genuine peace.

One painted a landscape with a mountain lake—calm, quiet, tranquil, serene, unperturbed. The background setting was one of beautiful green hills, ringed by tall slender pine trees reflected in the mirror-like surfaces of the lake.

The second artist painted a very turbulent scene with a violent waterfall crashing down on jagged chunks of granite rock. But alongside the waterfall was a slender birch tree, with its fragile branches reaching just above the crashing foam. And in the fork of one of the branches was a bird's nest. In the nest lying very calmly and serenly, glistening from the spray and the foam of the waterfall, was a small bird fast asleep. That is an accurate rendition of peace.

This second artist captured the feeling of peace that can be ours in the kind of world and life in which we have to live. God does not promise us there will be no problems. There will always be difficulties and problems, but God has promised that it is really possible for us to experience PEACE—real PEACE—in the midst of life!

Lord, I take my eyes off my problems and difficulties and turn them to You. As I do I can feel Your peace within me, a calmness in the midst of the storms of life!

Lovingly Forgive

"Be kind to each other, tenderhearted, forgiving one another, just as God has forgiven you because you belong to Christ."

Ephesians 4:32

Number six on my list of seven dynamic human values is FORGIVENESS. Someone looking at my list asked, "Why haven't you included *love?*" My answer is that the word *love* at its depth, really means FORGIVENESS.

The Greeks had three words for love. The richest word was *agape*, which is unlike any other word used for love. *Agape* means to love somebody even when they do not deserve to be loved. And that's the kind of love that God has for you and me. The interesting thing is *agape* can also be translated "to forgive!"

St. Paul writes, "While we were yet sinners Christ died for us" (Romans 5:8 KJV). That means very simply that God loved us even when He had no reason to. That's what agape means. That's what *grace* means. And that's what *forgiveness* means. It is God's love in action for people who do not deserve it!

I was taught that only God can truly forgive. Nature does not forgive. If, in a fit of anger I cut off a hand, it isn't going to grow back. Educators do not forgive. If I do not study for an exam, I will flunk. Society does not forgive. If I commit a crime, I must pay for it and my record will follow me every place I go. Forgiveness is a miracle only God can perform! And the cause of His forgiveness is His great love—*agape* love. I can be lovingly forgiven!

I live today without fear or guilt for God has lovingly forgiven me!

Lovingly Forgive

*"What happiness for those whose guilt has been forgiven!
What joys when sins are covered over! What relief for
those who have confessed their sins and God has cleared
their record."*

Psalm 32:1, 2

When God forgives, God forgets! Someone once said
that when you bury the hatchet, don't leave the handle
above the ground. You can always find the hatchet again
that way, and dig it up again. God never digs up our past
when he forgives! Isn't that beautiful! I am set free by
God's loving forgivness.

Reflect a moment on what that tremendous thought can
mean for you. Finish the following sentence as many times
as possible.

BECAUSE GOD FORGIVES ME, I CAN _____

_____

_____

_____

_____

_____

_____

_____

**I feel confident, strong and excited
because I am forgiven. Today I will live
in the joy of my forgiveness!**

Lovingly Forgive

"But God showed his great love for us by sending Christ to die for us while we were still sinners."

Romans 5:8

Forgiveness is non-judgmental love. I recall the doctor that spoke at the World Psychiatric Congress on the value of love. He told us the only real love is a non-judgmental love.

Most people love judgmentally: I'll love you if you agree with me politically. I'll love you if you'll start living a cleaner life. If you don't meet my expectations, I will not love you.

But St. Paul tells us that even when we were the enemies of God, He loved us non-judgmentally. There are no "ifs" in God's love for you and me!

In the Sermon on the Mount, Jesus said that if we love only the people that agree with us, what is so great about that? Even scoundrels and crooks love their fellow crooks. Jesus went on to say that genuine love is shown when God allows the sun to shine on the just and the unjust, and His rain falls on the good as well as the evil.

That may seem unjust to you, but let me assure you this concept is filled with mercy. And there will always be a tension between mercy and justice! If you are having difficulty forgiving someone because "what they did is just not right," let me encourage you to forgive as you have been forgiven.

> I can sense my anger and bitterness
> slipping away as I thank God for
> His forgiveness. I am forgiven.
> Therefore I am forgiving!

Lovingly Forgive

WHY FORGIVE? BECAUSE . . .

"Whatever a man sows, that he will also reap."
Galatians 6:7 RSV

"The measure you give will be the measure you get, and still more will be given to you."

Mark 4:24 RSV

"Your heavenly Father will forgive you if you forgive those who sin against you; but if you refuse to forgive them, he will not forgive you."

Matthew 6:15

"Give generously, for your gifts will return to you later."
Ecclesiastes 11:1

Lovingly Forgive

*"Be gentle and ready to forgive; never hold grudges.
Remember, the Lord forgave you, so you must forgive
others."*

Colossians 3:13

I submit that FORGIVENESS, as a human value, is the
most powerful healing force there is. Some of you are
carrying a grudge against someone, and you need forgiveness. Some of you may need to forgive yourself. And that
is the only way you will find healing for your sorrow, the
removal of jealousy, or the erasure of bitter memories.

Where in your life do you need the miraculous power of
forgivness? In a few words, identify the area of your life
where you need to experience forgiveness:

_____

_____

Now, in your mind imagine that you are approaching
the one whom you need to forgive. You explain the feelings
you have had and the need you now have to be forgiving.
In love, you ask forgiveness for not having been forgiving.
of them. Then imagine that you experience the warmth of
reconciliation. Enjoy that feeling, and then begin plans to
work out the above scene in real life.

God, in my own strength I cannot forgive.
But I am willing to be made willing.
Already, I am able to feel Your power at
work in me, helping me to forgive.

Lovingly Forgive

*"If we confess our sins to him, he can be depended on to
forgive us and to cleanse us from every wrong."*

1 John 1:9

Back in the 14th century, a monk announced to the
people of his village that he was going to preach the
greatest sermon ever preached on the Love of God. He
urged everyone to attend.

At the appropriate hour, the cathedral filled with the old
and the young. Throughout the service, everyone anticipated the great discourse. At the proper time, though, the
monk did not enter the pulpit, but instead went to the
candelabra, drew a long burning candle and then walked
high in the altar to the sculptured form of Christ nailed to
the cross.

He silently lifted the candle until the glow was directly
underneath one of the pierced hands. He held the candle
there with his back to the congregation.

Then he shifted and he held the candle below the other
pierced hand of Jesus. Slowly he moved the candle to the
side of our Lord where the spear had pierced Him. And
then he dropped to his knees in prayer, now holding the
glimmering light so that the glow fell on the nail-pierced
feet.

After a moment, the monk stood and turned, holding
the candle before him so that the people could see the
gentle tears on his face as he said, "My beloved people,
that is my sermon on the love of God for you." And he
dismissed them with a benediction!

> My heart is filled with love—
> God's love. I cannot help but
> be a forgiving person today!

Lovingly Forgive

"Love does not hold grudges."

1 Corinthians 13:5

As a boy, I loved the winter snows. But what we didn't appreciate were the blizzards, because they would come in with driving winds of 50 to 60 miles an hour and close the roads. We would be isolated on our farm. The only good thing about the blizzard was that I didn't have to go to school.

But soon we would look out down the road and see the snowplow coming, cutting through the drifts, slicing the snow, chopping it up and blowing it into a huge spewing stream in the ditch. And as the plow would pass, we were free to go to the store, and I could return to school.

Resentments are like snowdrifts and forgiveness is the snowplow. You see, in the eyes of many people, forgiveness is simply a matter of passive acquittal. But in the Christian context, forgiveness is a snowplow—opening the road, removing barriers, permitting communication to be restored.

There are a lot of resentments that can build up in our lives in the course of a day. And the only way to put joy on your face and in your heart is to find an overwhelming love that can remove resentments and fill you with FORGIVENESS.

"I forgive you" is the language of love!

> Today I speak the language of love.
> I am immune to resentments and
> grudges because I can lovingly forgive!

Hope!

"Why be discouraged and sad? Hope in God!

Psalm 42:5

HOPE is the seventh human value for dynamic living on my list. I recall the words of a prominent psychiatrist as he described the power in HOPE. He said, "All of us have had patients who sat in our offices, week after week, month after month, depressed, lifeless, dull, emotionally sick with skin sagging, eyes drooping, glassy and dull.

"Then came that moment in one of our counseling sessions when everything changed. We can't recall saying anything profound, and probably didn't, but we will never forget when the change took place.

"Suddenly the lifeless eyes come alive. The drooping eyelids open wide and the sparkle of life returns. The grey color of the skin changes as the whole person is suddenly alive and alert to life! Why? Because hope has returned.

"And what is hope? How can we as doctors define this emotion, where it comes from and what it does to a person? We can only call it a human phenomenon."

I know what that doctor was talking about and I know how to define the powerful spirit of hope that can change a person so dramatically. Call this spirit of hope by the right name—call it GOD! Hope is God's Spirit coming into a human being to change their life and perspective!

I am certain you have heard the sentence, "Where there is life, there is hope." I want you to permanently change that sentence to, *"Where there is hope, there is life!"*

I know that God is planning something good for me today!

Hope!

"Be joyful in hope."

Romans 12:12 (NIV)

I was in Calcutta, India a couple of years ago visiting with a friend. While there, I went to visit a place that I had been hearing about for some time—Mother Teresa's "Home for the Dying."

When Mother Teresa saw people dying in the streets of Calcutta, she was so moved that on her own, she dragged their dying bodies into a deserted temple which she had cleaned up. There she provided loving care. "Every human being at least deserves to have somebody loving them while they are dying." she said.

When I arrived at the home, the place was filled. There were narrow, low ceilings and dim lights, but everything smelled clean and sweet. One of the nurses told me: "Dr. Schuller, an interesting thing is happening. We accept only those people who are dying of some terminal disease. But, the amazing thing is that when they come here and feel the love of Christ, they are filled with hope and many of them stop dying. In fact, we're thinking of changing our name to the "Home for the Living!"

An incredible place and a perfect example of the statement—Where there's hope, there's life! There is tremendous power in HOPE!

**I am filled with joyful hope.
Life is exciting!**

Hope!

"And we know that all that happens to us is working for our good if we love God and are fitting into his plans."
Romans 8:28

Everywhere I go, I meet people who tell me, "My life has been changed!" And it is because there is change that there can be hope! Whatever your circumstances are today, it will change. Tomorrow will be different. And the amazing thing is that you can choose how your tomorrow will be different.

Think about that for a moment and then write down how you would like tomorrow to be different: _____

_____

_____

_____

_____

_____

_____

_____

_____

_____

Now choose to believe that through God's power at work within you, the tomorrow you have described will be yours.

Today I begin anew!

Hope!

"Let everything alive give praise to the Lord! You praise Him! Hallelujah!"

Psalm 150:6

What do you do when all hope seems gone? Especially when you *feel* hopeless? I find the Psalms a great source of help at these times.

Right now, try reading Psalm 146 through 150. They are short enough to read in one sitting. Then, after you have read these five short Psalms, add your own thoughts:

Praise the Lord, all you _____

_____!

Praise Him for _____

_____

_____!

I will praise Him with _____

_____

_____!

Congratulations, you've just written Psalm 151. Now, when feelings of hopelessness start to come, shut them off by re-reading your Psalm of praise!

I am praising God. As I am filled with praise, I am also filled with hope!

Hope!

"What is faith? Is it the confident assurance that some-thing we want is going to happen. Is it the certainty that what we hope for is waiting for us, even though we cannot see it up ahead."

Hebrews 11:1

Do you know what the alternative to HOPE is? Despair! I am amazed at how often men express the feelings of hope-lessness—despair.

In 1801, Wilberforce said that he dared not marry because the future was too unsettled.

In 1806, William Penn said, "There is scarcely anything around us but ruin and despair."

In 1848, Lord Shaftsbury said, "Nothing can save the British Empire from shipwreck."

In 1849, Benjamin Disraeli said, "In industry, commerce, and agriculture there is no hope."

In 1852, the dying Duke of Wellington said, "I thank God that I shall be spared from seeing the consummation of ruin that is settling in around us."

And in 1914, Lord Grey said, "The lamps are going out all over Europe; we shall not see the lite again in our lifetime."

Prominent experts of international repute have an amazing inclination to spread despair. Apparently they have never discovered the secret shared by the prophet Jeremiah: "My soul claims the Lord as my inheritance; therefore I will hope in Him" (Lamentations 3:24).

> **I choose to hope in God and I feel surrounded with His presence!**

Hope!

"But blessed is the man who trusts in the Lord and has made the Lord his hope and confidence."

Jeremiah 17:7

You are filled with HOPE! But as you look around, you see friends who are filled with despair and hopelessness. Stop a moment and consider which friend might need your encouragement today. Write down their first name: _____

From your perspective, why are they filled with despair?

_____

Write down some words of encouragement and hope that you can share with this person today, either in person or in writing. Remember, hope is nourished by affirming the possibilities available. Keep your encouragements on a positive note: _____

_____

_____

_____

_____

_____

_____

_____

> Because I have hope, I can be a messenger of hope to someone else today. That gives me a greater awareness of hope in my own life!

Hope!

"And so, Lord, my only hope is in you."

Psalm 39:7

Robert Louis Stevenson was a sickly child who never forgot his childhood experience of watching the old lamplighter coming down his street in Edinburgh, Scotland. Every night, the faithful man would come, lighting the oil lamps one-by-one as darkness began to approach.

In his later years, Stevenson remarked, "What I remember most about that lamplighter each night was that he always left a light behind him! And the light was a guide to those that followed afterwards."

What's the most beautiful sight in the world? A sunset? A snowcapped mountain peak? Confucius, the Chinese philosopher, is quoted as saying, "The most beautiful sight in the world is a little child going confidently down the road after you have shown him the way." The greatest joy in the world is to point someone who is lost in the right direction! You and I can do that!

When people ask me why I have hope in this life, I take them by the hand, point them to Christ and say, "There's the reason. Jesus gave me pardon, a purpose and hope!" "And the Lord will guide you continually, and satisfy you with all good things, and keep you healthy too; and you will be like a well-watered garden, like an ever-flowing spring." (Isaiah 58:11).

> **I believe that whatever happens to me today will prove to be a beautiful blessing!**

New Life

"And I will give you a new heart—I will give you new and right desires—and put a new spirit within you. I will . . . give you new hearts of love."

Ezekiel 36:26

On our church campus, we have a large number of walnut trees. In the fall the walnut trees drop their leaves. Those that don't fall off are blown off by what we call in California—the Santa Ana winds. These are strong winds that periodically come whipping through Southern California.

I was walking through our barren walnut grove the other day, and I saw here and there a dead leaf still clinging to the branch. The strong winds hadn't blown them off. The winter rains hadn't washed them off.

Sometimes we have problems like that. They just seem to hang on and the winds will not blow them off. The storms will not wash them off. But wait—in a little while new sap will come from the deep roots, surging through the trunk into the branches and a new bud will push the dead leaf off. *Every dead leaf that still clings on through the wintertime is doomed because new life will push it off in the spring!*

Depressed? Deflated? Defeated? New life can come to you! But you can't do it alone. Jesus said, "I am the Vine, you are the branches." (John 15:5). He is the life—He will push off the old and make room for the new.

> **Every day I am being renewed through the life and power of Jesus Christ.**

New Life

"When someone becomes a Christian he becomes a brand new person inside. He is not the same anymore. A new life has begun! All these new things are from God . . ."

2 Corinthians 5:17, 18

Where are the new buds in your life? Where is new life surging within you? I believe every problem is really an opportunity for God to work miracles. Describe a pressing problem and then write down all the potential opportunities for God to work a miracle.

My problem is _____

_____

_____

_____

God's opportunities for miracles are _____

_____

_____

_____

_____

I am praising God for my problems which are opportunities hiding God's great possibilities!

New Life

"Light dawns for the righteous, and joy for the upright in heart."

Psalm 97:11 RSV

Early one morning I went for a long run. I came to an intersection where I could keep on going east, turn to the south, or head north. If I turned south I would have a view of the breaking of the dawn over the ocean. If I headed north I would catch a view of the mountains in the breaking sunlight. Both options were tempting.

If I kept running east, I would be running up a slight hill. But I would be running toward what was a growing golden glow. I knew I would catch the daybreak, and I would feel the first long shafts of golden sunlight falling on my chilled face.

I started running toward the ocean, but I found I was running with my back to the daybreak, and that was disappointing. I felt I would be missing out on something beautiful.

So I had an easy decision. I turned to the east and *I ran to the sunrise!* And I was not disappointed. When I reached the top of the hill, the sun broke over the horizon and the bursting light was like being born anew.

How do you run to the light? You run to the light of God's Word!

Lord, I am running to your sunrise.
I am thinking about you.
I am being warmly blessed—right now!

New Life

"Choose to love the Lord your God and to obey him and to cling to him, for he is your life . . .!"

Deuteronomy 30:20

All of the great people in the Bible were possibility thinkers. Oh, they were realists—they knew what it was to be discouraged, depressed or on the verge of defeat. But they were great because even in the midst of their troubles, they chose to turn their attention to God's beautiful possibilities for their todays.

Even Jeremiah, the weeping prophet, in the depths of great depression finally chose to focus on God's great love. When he did, his depression left him (Read Lamentations 3:1-24). He chose to look at God's possibilities rather than pay attention to the negative forces surrounding him.

Are you troubled today? Do you feel that life is closing in on you and there is no way to escape? Don't let your mind dwell on negative thoughts. Choose life! Believe in God's ability to overcome the troubles and give you a great and exciting today. God's message to you is, "I know the plans I have for you . . . plans for good and not for evil, to give you a future and a hope." (Jeremiah 29:11).

> **I am choosing life—God's life.**
> **Therefore, I have nothing to fear.**

New Life

"The steadfast love of the Lord never ceases, his mercies never come to an end; they are new every morning; great is thy faithfulness."

Lamentations 3:22, 23 RSV

Psalm 148 encourages *everything* to praise the Lord—even the mountains and the trees. Today, make your own praise-list. If you need more space, start a praise notebook. When negative thoughts attack you, read over your praise list. Praise the Lord!

Begin by listing no less than 8 blessings for which you are grateful.

I praise the Lord for:

1. _____

2. _____

3. _____

4. _____

5. _____

6. _____

7. _____

8. _____

Now, keep adding to your list.

**Today Lord, I am praising You.
You are my ray of hope!**

New Life

"We are already God's children, right now, and we can't even imagine what it is going to be like later on. But we do know this, that when he comes we will be like him, as a result of seeing him as he really is."

1 John 3:2

This story is told about one of America's favorite entertainers—Dick Van Dyke. One night in his Arizona home, he and a number of guests were playing the game: "Who-I'd-Like-Most-To-Be." One person wanted to be Beethoven. Someone else said they would like to be Rockefeller. And so it went. When it came around to Dick Van Dyke, he hesitated, and sincerely, but shyly explained, "I don't want to sound silly," he admitted, "but I'd like most to be Christ."

That excites me because I agree with his choice! For Jesus Christ is the greatest possibility thinker who has ever lived! He really should have been an impossibility thinker—he had every reason. He was a minority, a citizen of an oppressed land, uneducated, poor and untraveled. Along with all of this, he served with little thanks.

He knew the secret! Looking at his disciples, he shared with them the secret when he said, "With men this is impossible, but with God all things are possible." (Matthew 19:26 RSV). Sharing God's new life makes you one of God's possibility people!

**Christ lives within me now.
I am one of His possibility people!**

New Life

"I can do everything God asks me to with the help of Christ who gives me the strength and power."

Philippians 4:13

You started the week with a choice and the encouragement to choose life! Now let's evaluate. Think back over the week and write down situations where you made life-generating, life-rendering, life-revitalizing decisions.

_____

_____

_____

God loves you and forgives you when you make wrong decisions. Accept His forgiveness as you commit the coming week to Him. Write down your commitment and refer to it during the coming week.

_____

_____

_____

_____

_____

> **Thank you Lord, I now feel Your strength and power enabling me to do anything You ask me to do.**

The Star of Joy

" . . . for the joy of the Lord is your strength."

Nehemiah 8 : 10

JOY—what is it? Write down your definition of joy:

_____

_____

_____

Your definition probably described some emotions or feelings that reflect an inner buoyancy. When you are filled with the joy of the Lord, your faith is strong. Nothing can discourage or defeat you. The prophet Nehemiah understood this when he told the people to celebrate, ". . . for the joy of the Lord is your strength."

A strong faith is built on the joy of the Lord. And where there is joy, there is room only for the positive things in life.

My definition of joy? Jesus first, Others second, Yourself last. Unselfishness is the key to personal happiness.

> **My faith is strong because I am filled with the joy of the Lord now.**

The Star of Joy

"Thou wilt shew me the path of life; in thy presence is fulness of joy; at thy right hand there are pleasures for evermore."

Psalm 16:11 KJV

There are five points in the Star of Joy.

The first point of the star is *Conceive*. When Jesus Christ comes into your life, He fills your heart with the love that will produce JOY. But you must first *conceive* of the fact that it is possible for Christ to come into your life.

Perhaps you underestimate your faith. Take the time now and write down what you really truly believe about God—Jesus—Love.

God _____

_____

Jesus _____

_____

Love _____

_____

Now take the psalmist at his word. He said that God will show you the path of life. Believe that with the help of God's Holy Spirit you can now *conceive*, imagine, and visualize Christ's coming into your mind and heart. Great joy comes when you begin to *conceive* that it is possible for God to come into your life. It's possible!

> **Lord, I feel Christ's spirit coming in my mind now. I believe it is possible for Him to live within me.**

The Star of Joy

"But to all who received him, who believed in his name, he gave power to become children of God."

John 1:12 RSV

The first point of the star is *Conceive*. The second point of the star of joy is *Receive*. God's wonderful book—the Bible—makes it very clear that if you ask Jesus Christ to come into your life, He will do it. Now I can't completely explain this reality scientifically, psychologically or any other way, but it is a fact. The Bible teaches it. Try it! It works!

Through thoughts about Christ, and through ideas about Jesus that come into your mind, Christ comes into your life. Through an experience with Christ—and a love for Christ—He comes into your life.

If you have never done this before, take the time now to invite Jesus Christ into your life. *Receive* Him and let the very living mind of Christ reach into your mind and life.

Whether you have just invited Christ into your life now, or have invited Him in before, take the space below and describe what it means to you to be a child of God:

_____

_____

_____

Christ lives within me now!

The Star of Joy

"May the God of hope fill you with all joy and peace in believing, so that by the power of the Holy Spirit you may abound in hope."

Romans 15:13 RSV

The third point of the star is *Believe*. After you have conceived of the facts and received Christ into your life, don't expect rockets to explode. Simply *believe*.

Those early Christians in the book of Acts saw trouble erupt in their lives when they believed, but they were filled with joy. God does not promise that your eyes will fill up with tears or that your heart will burst with emotion. This may happen. However, joy comes to you when you believe, because God promises to act on your faith.

When our faith is weak, our joy fades. Are you experiencing doubts? Identify them. Write them down. Then change them into affirmations and watch your joy begin to shine brightly again.

Your doubt	Your affirmation
IS CHRIST IN MY LIFE?	I HAVE RECEIVED CHRIST INTO MY LIFE AND I BELIEVE HE IS THERE NOW!

The Star of Joy

"Since we have been made right in God's sight by faith in his promises, we can have real peace with him because of what Jesus Christ our Lord has done for us."

Romans 5:1

Point four is *Relieve*. Joy comes when you *relieve* yourself and your mind from all negative thoughts. Fear, hate, doubt, suspicion, hostility, unbelief—all of these are negative forces that rob you of joy. Faith does not harmonize with any of these negative emotions, so relieve your mind of them.

I recall the time that one small dead spider in the thermostat at the base of the stairs in our sanctuary knocked out our whole air conditioning system one Sunday.

If a dead spider can do that, what do you think one prejudice, or one hate, or one worry that you hang on to can do? Joy fills the vacuum left when you *relieve* your mind of negative thoughts.

Saint Paul understood this. He wrote, "Fix your thoughts on what is true and good and right. Think about things that are pure and lovely, and dwell on the fine, good things in others. Think about all you can praise God for and be glad about." (Philippians 4:8). Memorize this verse. When negative thoughts press in on you, repeat this affirmation until your mind is clear and open to God and His goodness.

I relieve my mind of negative thoughts by thinking of good things.

The Star of Joy

"Brethren, I do not consider that I made it on my own; but one thing I do, forgetting what lies behind and straining forward to what lies ahead, I press on toward the goal . . ."

Philippians 3:13 RSV

And now point five—*Actchieve*. I've deliberately misspelled the word achieve—ACT-chieve. That's the key!

ACT! Be like a sprinkler head and let the water of joy flow through. Be like a fountain pen and let Christ, like beautiful ink, write his message through your life.

What are your dreams? What would you like to achieve? What could you do that would bring you great joy? Do it! Dare to be a dreamer and then dare to ACT!

Write down one of your dreams, that if accomplished would bring you joy: _____

_____

_____

Now write down the first thing you would have to do to ACT-chieve your dream—and then do it with God's help.

_____

_____

_____

> Lord, I look at my dream and I will never be a quitter. Thank you for the strength and patience to act-chieve my dream, for I believe it is Your dream also.

The Star of Joy

"I have told you this so that you will be filled with my joy. Yes, your cup of joy will overflow!"

John 15:11

Our Star of Joy—it is only complete when all five points are there. Joy is present when we Conceive, Receive, Believe, Relieve, and ACT-chieve. It takes all five. Live by them and Christ's joy will fill you to overflowing!

Which point of the star is weakest in your life? Write down how you would like that point to be. For example, perhaps you find it difficult to *Relieve* your mind of negative thoughts and this destroys your joy. Write down what you would like your thought life to be like.

_____

_____

_____

_____

_____

Now take some time today and share with a friend or a member of your family, your definition of joy, and what you are going to do to increase the joy of the Lord in your life.

The joy of the Lord is my strength!

Follow the Leader

"Yes, be bold and strong! Banish fear and doubt! For remember, the Lord your God is with you wherever you go."

Joshua 1:9

Olympic champion Charley Paddock was speaking to the young men at East Tech High School. "If you think you can, you can!" he challenged the youths. "If you believe a thing strongly enough, it can come to pass in your life!"

Afterward a spindly-legged boy said to Mr. Paddock, "Gee Sir, I'd give anything if I could be an Olympic champion just like you!" It was that lad's moment of inspiration. His life changed. In 1936 that young man went to Berlin, Germany, to compete in the Olympics. He came home with four gold medals! His name—Jesse Owens.

Back home he was driven through the streets of Cleveland to the cheers of the crowd. The car stopped and he signed some autographs. A skinny little boy pressed against the car and said, "Gee, Mr. Owens, I'd give anything to be an Olympic champ like you!" Jesse reached out and put his hand on the boy's arm as he said, "You know, young fellow, I was about your age when I said the same thing. If you'll work and train and believe, you can be an Olympic champion!"

In 1948 at Wembly Stadium in London, England, that same little boy was a young man. He crouched waiting for the starter's gun to go off for the finals of the 100-meter dash. Harrison "Bones" Dillard won the race and tied Jesse Owen's Olympic record!

Everyday, people are being inspired to greatness by the example of someone else. Who's your inspiring leader?

> **I am enthusiastic. I am alert!**
> **I am ready to follow God's leadership!**

Follow the Leader

". . . The man who finds life will find it through trust-ing God."

Galatians 3:11

All of us have been inspired to do something through someone else's example. Sometimes it is only a word or two that catches our attention and changes the direction of our lives. Other times, it is the example of someone over a period of time that provides inspiration for our thinking.

When my uncle returned from China on furlough as a missionary, he visited our Iowa farm. I was only four years old, but I still remember his words to me at the gate. "Bob," he said, "you're going to be a preacher!" That moment changed the direction of my life.

As you think back over your life, who have been the people that have influenced you? Whether by a chance encounter or a long-term relationship, who has influenced your decisions? Stop and think a moment and then write down their names:

NAME   EVENT

_____   _____

_____   _____

_____   _____

_____   _____

Now thank God for the lives and example of each of these people. Maybe you could drop one of them a note thanking them for the example they provided for your life.

> I am thankful for the people God is sending into my life. They are his messengers to me!

Follow the Leader

"O Lord, I will honor and praise your name, for you are my God; you do such wonderful things!"

Isaiah 25:1

What makes a person a leader? What qualities make one person a leader and another person a follower? What qualities do you look for in a boss, a president, or any other person who, at one time or another, is a leader in your life?

Make a list of what you consider to be leadership qualities.

A LEADER IS:

1. _____

2. _____

3. _____

4. _____

Now read Isaiah 53 over again. In this passage, the great prophet is speaking about Jesus Christ. Make a list of the characteristics Isaiah says Jesus would have.

THE MESSIAH, JESUS, WOULD BE:

1. _____

2. _____

3. _____

4. _____

How do your lists compare?

> **I am one with Christ.
> I willingly follow Him!**

Follow the Leader

"My constant boast is God. I can never thank you enough!"

Psalm 44:8

Today, Jesus Christ literally lives in millions of human beings around the world. He lives in my life. He has been and continues to be the most influential leader in the history of the human race. Yet He had every reason to be an impossibility thinker.

For example, He was a member of a minority race, who at that time were an oppressed people. His native countrymen were under the rule of the Romans. Taxes were oppressive. They had no political freedom. Yet He seemingly did nothing about those conditions.

He was uneducated. He had no academic degrees or diplomas. Moreover, poverty was His lot all His life. He never owned a home of His own. He Himself said, "Foxes have holes, birds of the air have nests. I have nothing."

He came from the low-class uncultured people. His father was a common laborer. High-brow critics said of his origin, "Can anything good come out of Nazareth?"

He never married and was isolated from men of power and influence. He had no powerful connections in the local government. His own band of followers were ragged, rugged, unpolished losers.

He served other people all his life and received little thanks for what He did. In the end, He became the innocent victim of a massive injustice. His friends let Him down and one of them even betrayed Him.

In the end, he even felt forsaken by God. He had every reason to give up, but instead, He changed the whole course of history!

> **I am one with Christ.**
> **I am in tune with His will!**

Follow the Leader

"Your attitude should be the kind that was shown to us by Jesus Christ."

Philippians 2:5

Instead of becoming bitter, cynical, angry, negative, or a furious revolutionary, Jesus willingly died on a cross to pay the penalty of man's rebellion against God. He rose from the dead, victorious over sin and death. Today, He offers life and hope for all who will believe.

To Jesus, problems were possibilities in disguise. Sick people were an opportunity to perform a miracle and show God's love. Even on the cross, He took the opportunity to take care of His mother and the dying thief next to Him.

All persons had hidden possibilities. A rough and tough Peter, a cheap prostitute named Mary, a crooked tax collector named Zacchaeus—all had goodness waiting to be brought out! He purposely sought out the problem people. Those whom the world would blackball, He courted and converted!

He believed in the dignity of the individual. So He never called a person a sinner. He always saw the individual as a saint. But He also believed in ultimate justice. Eternity would even accounts. So He had as much to say about Hell as he He did about Heaven.

The immeasurable mercy of God was still another great possibility that He proclaimed. He promised that any sin could be forgiven if we would repent.

> Christ in me is changing my attitudes.
> I am becoming more positive every day
> in every area of my life!

Follow the Leader

"Jesus Christ is the same yesterday, today, and forever."
Hebrews 13:8

Jesus said,
"I am the Good Shepherd. The Good Shepherd lays down his life for the sheep."

John 10:11

"I am the Gate. Those who come in by way of the Gate will be saved and will go in and out and find green pastures."
John 10:9

"I am the Bread of Life. No one coming to me will ever be hungry again. Those believing in me will never thirst."
John 6:35

"I am the Vine; you are the branches. Whoever lives in me and I in him shall produce a large crop of fruit."

John 15:5

"I am the Way—yes, and the Truth and the Life. No one can get to the Father except by means of me."

John 14:6

"I am the one who raises the dead and gives them life again. Anyone who believes in me, even though he dies like anyone else, shall live again!"

John 11:25

"I have come as a Light to shine in this dark world, so that all who put their trust in me will no longer wander in the darkness."

John 12:46

Follow the Leader

"And those who are wise—the people of God—shall shine as brightly as the sun's brilliance, and those who turn many for righteousness will glitter like stars forever."
                                                    Daniel 12:3

The most important question of your life is—"What do you think of Jesus Christ?" The Roman commander in charge of His execution turned away and was heard saying, "Truly this man was the Son of God!"

What do you think? Is He alive at the center of your life? Have you ever invited Jesus Christ into your life as your Savior? If not, I encourage you to choose Him as your leader. Turn over the control of your life to the only one who can give you a fresh new beginning. Pray this prayer:

"Lord Jesus Christ, I am discovering that many things are possible that I never before believed were possible. I am becoming aware of the fact that you want to live within me guiding and helping me as I live each day. I believe that you were sent by your Father into this world to become my Savior. I asked you to forgive me and change me. I accept you now. Thank you, Lord. Amen."

Now that you have discovered the power of Jesus Christ in your life, you will want to tell someone else the good news! What special person in your life would be interested in knowing about God's good news? Call them, or write them a letter sharing what you discovered this week about Jesus Christ.

> The joy of Jesus Christ is mine. He is my leader. I am becoming a better, more positive person because Jesus Christ lives within me!

Jesus Is Lord

*"No one can say, "Jesus is Lord," and really mean it, unless
the Holy Spirit is helping him."*

1 Corinthians 12:3

Do you dare to trust God? Jesus did. As He made His
triumphant entry into the city of Jerusalem, Jesus was
saying to all the people, "I dare to trust My Father who is
in Heaven." He dared to trust God even when He knew
how costly that decision would be!

It is interesting to see how kings have made their
Portugal, England, Austria, or Prussia you will have seen
magnificent, splendid carriages carved out of fascinating
woods. The fenders and corners of the hoods and the
covers of the carriages are adorned with carved cupids,
then entirely overlaid with gold! The kings rode into their
cities in these gold-plated, cupid-carved chariots.

Roll back the centuries and watch the Roman emperors
as they enter riding in golden chariots drawn by six or eight
stallions. As they enter the city, the streets are cleared for
two miles. What pomp! What excitement!

Then there was Caesar. He had to be different, so his
chariot was drawn by six tawny lions. Pompey used
elephants to pull his chariot.

And then there was Jesus—King of Israel and Lord of all
creation! He entered His capital city riding on a donkey!
No pomp, no show, no lofty pride, just love in His face!

**Jesus, Your love draws me
closer to You this day!**

Jesus Is Lord

"There is peace with God through Jesus, the Messiah, who is Lord of all creation."

Acts 10:36

Who was this Jesus, who came into Jerusalem riding on a donkey? The crowds cried, "Hosanna: Blessed is the King of Israel that cometh in the name of the Lord" (John 12:13 KJV). Yet a little later this same week, they are crying out, "Crucify him!"

Perhaps the most profound question in all of history is: What do you think of Jesus? Think a moment and then either write down your ideas, make a list, draw a picture, or do something below that expresses your attitude towards Jesus.

**My thoughts are focused on Jesus.
I feel His spirit within!**

Jesus Is Lord

*"Great and marvelous are your doings, Lord God
Almighty. Just and true are your ways, O King of Ages."*
                                                    Revelations 15:3

A poet once wrote,
> "So lowly does the Savior ride
> On a paltry borrowed beast.
> No pomp, no show, no lofty pride,
> No board above the leaf.
> His scepter is His kindness,
> His grandeur is His grace,
> His royalty, holiness.
> Love is in His face.
> 'Twas thus the great Messiah came
> To break the tyrant's will.
> To heal the people of their shame
> And nobleness instill.
> Ride on, Oh King, ride on your way.
> Ride on, Jesus, now, today."

Why was He crucified? If He was gentle, kind, noble and
loving, why did they crucify Him? For one simple reason:
The people expected Him to lead a revolution. They
expected Him to be the radical that would drive the
Romans out and set Israel free!

But Jesus was not interested in politics. He was there to
change hearts and bring NEW LIFE to you and me!
Let Him be Lord! Allow Jesus to be Himself—the Lord God
Almighty.

**Lord, forgive me for trying to make You
into something less than You are. I
worship You as King—my King—today!**

Jesus Is Lord

"For this is my blood, sealing the New Covenant. It is poured out to forgive the sins of multitudes."

Matthew 26:28

When you allow Jesus Christ to come into sharp focus in the core of your mind, a fire goes on—the fire of the Holy Spirit of the living God. You are turned from negative to positive, and that's exciting!

The positive idea that Jesus expressed as He sat to eat with His disciples is so simple that we often are inclined to ignore it. It sounds like old hat, but it's as revolutionary as tomorrow! The idea is the powerful, positive idea of love, *love*, LOVE!

What gets me so excited is that until the coming of Jesus Christ, there was no form of worship or religion that really was centered in love. The Old Covenant in the Old Testament was centered on the law. The emphasis was on obedience and regular blood sacrifices for the atonement of sin. It was not love, even though it was very loving.

But Jesus said he marked the beginning of the New Covenant. And the New Covenant of Love answers the two most important questions and any person can ask:

What can I expect from God?

What does God expect from me?

And the answer to both questions is the same—LOVE! God's grace is so great that He loves me even when I don't deserve it. And everything leading up to the cross and the crucifixion is the evidence of God's unfailing, unlimited and sacrificial love for you and me! That's the message of the New Covenant!

> **I invite the transforming love of God to do its work in me!**

Jesus Is Lord

*"Even when walking through the dark valley of death I will
not be afraid, for you are close beside me, guarding,
guiding all the way."*

Psalm 23:4

By all the laws of known psychological development,
Jesus Christ should have become the world's greatest
impossibility thinker. He was a member of despised
minority, a citizen of an occupied country, a Jew, and the
world hated the Jews.

With the racial prejudice He experienced as a child, He
should have grown up to be oversensitive, touchy and
defensive. Taxes were oppressive. Freedom was limited.
Survival was uncertain. Religion was in the minor key—
restrictive, negative and joyless.

Yet Jesus never grew up to make an inflammatory
speech, never organized a guerilla force in the mountains
and never led a march on Rome.

He was uneducated, untravelled and unhonored. He did
not know the politicians, or the other "important" people
of His day. In fact, it was said of Him, "Look how he
attracts the losers, not the influential."

He lived and died in poverty. He had no home of His
own, no insurance or retirement plan, and no wife to com-
fort Him. But by the miracle of miracles, He grew up to be
the World's Greatest Possibility Thinker!

He believed in and proved the ultimate possibilities, such
as: "I am the resurrection and the life. He who lives and
believes in me shall never die!" And when He died, *He rose
again!* And through His death, He lives to give life and
meaning to each of us!

> **I live because Jesus lives!**

Jesus Is Lord

*"I will give him the honors of one who is mighty and great,
because he has poured out his soul unto death."*

Isaiah 53:12

What does the cross mean in your life? We wear gold or
silver crosses around our neck as a symbol of our faith. We
place crosses on steeples of churches and in the front of our
sanctuaries. But for Jesus, the cross was an instrument of
suffering, pain and death.

The tremendous possibilities of our faith is how God can
take a cruel instrument of death and turn it into a symbol
of hope and life.

Think for a moment about the possibilities available to
you today because of the cross of Jesus Christ. Describe the
meaning of the cross in your life today.

THE CROSS OF JESUS CHRIST MEANS _____

_____

_____

_____

_____

_____

_____

In the cross of Christ I glory—not for its
cruelty but for the hope and possibilities
it symbolizes!

Jesus Is Lord

"As for me, God forbid that I should boast about anything except the cross of our Lord Jesus Christ."

Galatians 6:14

Towering high above the converging freeways in Orange County is the 100 foot tall cross sitting on top of the Tower of Hope. Rising over 250 feet above the ground, it is a light that shines continuously—symbolizing the hope promised by Jesus Christ.

Pilots landing at Orange County Airport tell me they use our cross as a reference point, making certain they are in the right landing path. People lying on hospital beds in the County Medical Center look out their window at the lighted cross. Many lives have been changed by its silent witness.

One night, just after midnight, a security guard making his rounds found a young woman lying unconscious in our parking lot. He called one of our NEW HOPE counselors, asking for them to come and check on her.

The counselor came downstairs just as she was starting to babble. They carried her upstairs and gave her some coffee and wrapped her in a warm blanket. For four hours, this counselor stayed with this girl until she was coherent. As she was leaving to receive medical attention, she said to the counselor. "I knew that if I could just get to the cross, I would find help!"

My friend, the cross is where each of us must come to find the answer to our deepest needs. At the cross, help is always available!

I come to the cross and I meet Jesus. He fills my soul with courage and strength.

Come-Alive-Power

"I am leaving you with a gift—peace of mind and heart! And the peace I give isn't fragile like the peace the world gives. So don't be troubled or afraid."

John 14:27

Even to a possibility thinker, there are some things that are impossible. For someone to stand at the beginning of a day and say to the sun, "Today you shall not make your sweeping sail through the sky," is an impossibility! Or for someone to go to the seashore and draw a line in the sand at low tide and say to the sea, "Today you shall not rise above this line" is an impossibility.

For the Roman soldiers to put a stone in front of the tomb where Jesus was laid and say, "You shall never rise again!" was an impossibility! In the same way, it is impossible for you to invite Christ into your life and not receive His *Come-Alive-Power!* The sun will shine, the tide will rise, CHRIST IS ALIVE AND WHEN He comes into your life, you will receive power!

Christ gives *Come-Alive-Power!* Perhaps some of you have never experienced this dynamic peace. It can happen! You can know this power in your life!

This week we will look at four words that describe the Come-Alive-Power that Jesus Christ gives when He transforms you. They are four simple words that you can easily remember.

First of all, *courage*. Second, you receive *confidence*. Third, you find *companionship*. And fourth, you discover the capacity for *communication!* When these four words are a reality in your life, then you have discovered *Come-Alive-Power!*

It is impossible for me not to know Christ's come-alive-power in my life today!

Come-Alive-Power

*"The Lord is my Helper and I am not afraid of anything
that mere man can do to me."*

Hebrews 13:6

Christ gives *courage!* Real dynamic courage. He
promises, "Peace give I to you!" And He can do this
because everyone knows Christ is no longer afraid of
dying. And when you have eliminated the fear of death,
you have eliminated the source of all fears.

Some time ago I was reading in the British annals when I
came across an interesting anecdote. There was a time in
the West Indies when there were five ships anchored in the
harbor. One was a British ship.

Suddenly an unexpected storm came up and the waves
rolled fiercely into the harbor. The British officer raised the
anchor and set his ship at sea directly into the mounting,
rolling waves. He sailed out of the harbor into the face of
the storm.

Two days later, battered and bruised, but still afloat and
intact, he came back to the harbor. In the calm that
hovered over the now still waters he surveyed the scene
and found that the other four ships that had not weighed
anchor for fear of the storm had been driven onto the shore
and destroyed!

There is only one way to conquer a fear and that is to
face it! If Christ is your Lord and God, you face any fear
without being afraid! *Come-Alive-Power gives courage!*

**In the storms of life, I face into the
wind—courageous because Jesus Christ
gives me the power!**

Come-Alive-Power

"Don't be afraid of them; don't be frightened . . ."
Ezekiel 2:6

Everyone needs courage! I need it; you need it. Stop a moment and look at your life. Where could you use courage today? What situation are you faced with that stirs up feelings of fear within you? Describe the situation briefly: _____

_____

_____

Christ's Come-Alive-Power gives you courage. Imagine in your mind how you would act in that situation, exercising the power of Jesus Christ to give you courage. Now describe how you *will* act with courage in that instance:

_____

_____

_____

_____

_____

I am courageous! I can feel Christ's
power in my life giving me courage.
I am no longer afraid!

Come Alive Power

"Abraham . . . was confidently waiting for God to bring him to that strong heavenly city whose designer and builder is God."

Hebrews 11:10

The second thing that Christ gives is *confidence!* Confidence eliminates the anxiety that comes from irresponsible liberty. Do you realize that today our country is one of the most anxiety-plagued societies in history? And this rise in anxiety comes in a period of time that we have, supposedly, more total freedom and liberty than ever before.

Psychologists have studied this. One test was made on a playground. The researchers felt that fences around playgrounds led to feelings of oppression, so for one group of students, they took down the fences—total freedom!

Guess what happened? The children became anxiety prone. They huddled together and played in the center of the playground. They didn't dare to run for fear that they might run into danger. But when the fences were put up again, they would race across the playground and run with their hands outstretched into the fence. Fences mean security! Especially when they are positive!

When Christ comes into your life, you have a new moral consciousness. You have fences. You say, "I will be true to Christ, to God and to those around me." And this gives *confidence!* You can face anyone unashamed. You have no dark secrets. And that produces confidence at the deepest possible level!

I have confidence that God is going to see me through this day, and each new day, because He lives within me!

Come-Alive-Power

"The greatest love is shown when a person lays down his life for his friends, and you are my friends if you obey me."
John 15:13, 14

We are plagued by loneliness today. Companionship is something we treasure. But some of us no longer know the beauty of a companion. We lack enthusiasm, happiness and joy because we suffer from loneliness and defeat. Inwardly we feel defeated and we dare not share it with anyone.

Some of us suffer from the loneliness of failure. We think we have failed at something and we dare not talk to anyone else about it. Others are successful and still suffer from loneliness. These people do not share their success because of the fear that others would think they are boasting. I don't know which is worse—the loneliness of failure or the loneliness of success.

Some suffer from the loneliness of sorrow. Alone in your grief you mourn for someone who is gone. Others suffer the loneliness of sickness and pain and may not even tell their spouse or their children how much it hurts. They simply suffer in the loneliness of silence.

There is only one cure for loneliness. And that is the realization that there is one companion who understands, truly understands you. Only Christ can come and save you from loneliness—that isolation of the spirit. He alone is the cure for that negative emotion. Our hearts are homesick for companionship with our creator. The Come-Alive-Power of Jesus Christ brings companionship!

I am not alone.
Jesus Christ is my constant companion!

Come-Alive-Power

"In response to all he has done for us, let us outdo each other in being helpful and kind to each other and in doing good."

Hebrews 10:24

When do you ever feel lonely? Describe what "lonely" means to you: _____

_____

_____

_____

Who are the lonely people around you? Think of several people who might be lonely. What could you do to ease their loneliness?

NAME	WHAT I COULD DO
_____	_____
_____	_____
_____	_____
_____	_____
_____	_____

Because Christ gives me come-alive-power, I am His instrument in easing loneliness in those around me!

Come Alive Power

"For Christ himself is our way of peace. He has made peace between us . . . making us all one family."

Ephesians 2:14

A few weeks ago I had to spank my youngest child, Gretchen. She's a darling girl, but she misbehaved and I had to punish her. She ran off to her room and closed the door behind her.

After a few minutes, I walked down the hall and listened at her door. Everything was so quiet so I turned the doorknob ever so slowly and peeked my head through the opening. There was her small figure hidden beneath the blankets.

As I walked over to the bed I noticed her treasured toys were scattered across the bed and cuddled next to her was her dolly. I stroked her hair and held her tear-stained face in my hands as I whispered, "Gretchen, are you awake?" She turned her head as she opened her eyes. Still hugging her dolly, I knew she wanted to hug her daddy.

"Gretchen," I explained, "I gave you that spanking because I love you." Her hands came out from under the covers, let go of the dolly, and reached up around my neck. As she put her slippery wet cheek next to mine, I prayed, "Dear God, thank you for Gretchen!" That tender moment was a time of special *communication* between us.

Jesus Christ is alive today and wants to communicate with you. He wants to love you, but you have to let go of your substitute. For a dolly is never a substitute for a daddy! Let Jesus Christ love you today!

I come to You, Lord, because
You understand me. I accept Your love.
I feel Your presence. I have
Your power within me!

Unlock the Gate

"But now is the time . . . Today if you hear God's voice speaking to you, do not harden your hearts against him."
                                                Hebrews 3:15

What's holding you back? By now you know there is:
> a goal you should be pursuing
> a dream you should be launching
> a plan you should be executing
> a project you should be starting
> a possibility you should be exploring
> an opportunity you should be grabbing
> an idea you should be working
> a problem you should be tackling
> a decision you should be making!

I say it's time to unlock the starting gate! NOW is the time to take action and STOP postponing. But what's holding you back? What are your favorite excuses for not beginning? Write them down:

I can't begin today because _____

_____

and because _____

_____

and also because _____

_____

> **I am enthusiastic and confident.
> I am ready for all that God
> has planned for me!**

Unlock the Gate

"Thank God! It has been done by Jesus Christ our Lord. He has set me free."

Romans 7:25

Frieda Schulze was 87 when I heard her story. At 77 years of age she took the plunge toward a new life. "I still shudder a bit when I think about it," Frau Schulze said, "But it was worth it . . . I couldn't stand their politics," she added, shaking a gnarled finger for emphasis.

When the East Germans built the wall in Berlin, Frau Schulze lived on the ground floor of an apartment house smack on the border. The sidewalk was West Berlin, but the apartment house was in East Berlin. The windows on the ground floor were bricked up after a number of people had escaped through them. The remaining residents were moved to the upper floor apartments.

"They moved me up, too, and when I got to the new place I sat there as if I were paralyzed," she remarked. She had no lights, but plenty of light from the searchlights outside. Her sleep was interrupted constantly with shots, sirens, the voices of West Berliners urging someone to escape and the vulgarities of the East German guards.

Finally, Frau Schulze had enough. She climbed out on her windowsill and was immediately spotted by West Berlin police. They called out the fire brigade with the nets and urged her to jump. Then she heard the door of her apartment kicked open and two East German guards grabbed her. Just then, a West Berlin policeman grabbed her ankle from below and both started to pull. Finally, she struggled free and jumped—to freedom. She opened the gate! It's never too late to begin!

**Jesus sets me free.
I begin today with a clean slate!**

Unlock the Gate

"My grace is sufficient for you, for my power is made perfect in weakness."

2 Cor. 12:9 RSV

Thomas Carlyle had finished his tremendous manuscript on the French Revolution. He gave it to his neighbor, John Stuart Mill, to read. Several days later, Mill came to Carlyle's home pale and nervous. His maid had used the manuscript to start a fire!

Carlyle was in a frenzy for days. Two years of labor lost. He could never muster the energy to write again. A task that large was overwhelming the first time. The thought of having to write the whole thing over was almost paralyzing.

One day, as Carlyle was walking the streets, he saw a stonemason building a long, high wall. He stood watching for a long time before he was suddenly impressed with the fact that the wall was being built *one brick at a time!* He took inspiration from that experience and decided, "I'll just write one page today, and then one page tomorrow. One page at a time—that's all I'll think about."

He started small and slow. The task was tedious, but he stayed with it and went on to finish the work. The end result was better than the first time!

Don't let bad memories or unfortunate incidents move in and dominate you. You can't get far looking in the rear-view mirror, you must look ahead!

> **God is mighty in the midst of me as I open myself to Him. I can do all things!**

Unlock the Gate

Deep within myself
I have a powerful awareness that
I have made the right decision
and am moving in the right direction.

I will let nothing and no one
deter, detour, distract, depress, or defeat me.
"No man having put his hand to the plow and
looking back is fit for the kingdom of God."

God's spirit is rising within me
now,
making me very determined
to faithfully keep the beautiful promises
I've made.
I will be faithful.
I am reliable.
Thank you, God.
Amen.

Unlock the Gate

"Forgetting the past and looking forward to what lies ahead, I strain to reach the end of the race and receive the prize for which God is calling us."

Philippians 3:13, 14

Have you had so many victories, successes and accomplishments that you're tired and you've decided to back off? Do you look at the trophies, the awards and the prizes of yesterday and lean on these laurels? A salesman told me, "I've gone downhill ever since I won the highest award my company can give in sales. I guess I was trying to prove something to someone and now I don't seem to care anymore."

How do you overcome feelings like that? Perhaps you feel that way even though you haven't been to the top—the struggle has been too difficult. Either way, I suggest you try letting God restimulate you. Read over the verse above several times. Let its meaning sink into your mind. Now rewrite the verse in your own words, relating it to your own situation:_____

_____

_____

_____

_____

Then remind yourself that *ease* will always lead to *disease*. As soon as you stop struggling, you lose your power. Press on!

There is a way! I am filled with power as I press forward!

Unlock the Gate

"If you wait for perfect conditions, you will never get anything done."

Ecclesiastes 11:4

Several years ago I disciplined myself to walk several miles each day. Then I fell off a ladder, was hospitalized for a short time and then restricted in any physical activity for several months. Of course, I got out of the rigorous self-disciplined habit of walking. To get myself going again, I mentally told myself that if I started walking again, I would keep my heart healthy, stay thinner, even look younger and maintain a good posture. Each reason added guilt, but still I put off walking.

Then one day my barber told me to wash my hair everyday for a week and take a walk to dry it. That did it! I had the extra prod to get started. Prior to that time I had good reasons to begin, but it took someone else to push me out the door and get started. My barber unlocked my starting gate!

Have you started yet? If you're still working at the beginning, build a sense of urgency into your thinking and get going. Just do a little bit—just enough to begin. Decide only to take that first step. Then decide to take the second step. And then the third. Now tell yourself, "I've got a great thing going—I must not stop!

Remember, the hardest part of any job is getting started. So what are you going to do today to get started?

_____

_____

> **Beginning is half done! Already I can feel energy flowing into me as I begin the creative task God has given me!**

Unlock the Gate

"For His Holy Spirit speaks to us deep in our hearts, and tells us that we really are God's children."

Romans 8:16

The human brain is made up of the cortex and the thalamus. The brain is like a walnut—the outside bark is the cortex. In fact, the word cortex means "bark." The inner part of the brain is the thalamus. Now the thalamus is the center of feeling and emotion, while the cortex is the intelligent, thinking part of you.

DON'T LET YOUR THALAMUS MANIPULATE YOUR CORTEX!

If your cortex—the thinking you—says, "It's a good idea," while your thalamus—the emotional you—objects saying, "I can't get in the mood," then in these situations, use your head! Use your cortex!

The thalamus is the inner nerve center and is the active part of the brain in a newborn child. It is the selfish, grasping brain that says, "I want what I want when I want it." If you are not doing what you know you should do, then your thalamus is running your cortex. The baby is running the adult. The emotions have the upper hand over your common sense.

This is true, not only about tasks you set for yourself, it also works in your relationship to Jesus Christ. If you have invited Jesus Christ into your life, there will be days when you do not *feel* like a child of God. Don't listen to your feelings. Listen to the facts—YOU ARE A CHILD OF GOD! Don't let your thalamus rule your cortex!

> **I keep my thoughts tuned to God.**
> **My attention is on His power.**

God's Presence

"When someone becomes a Christian he becomes a brand new person inside. He is not the same anymore. A new life has begun!

2 Corinthians 5:17

God's presence—behind you, in front of you and around you. You can feel it, know it, believe it, have it and hold on to it; you can face anything, anytime, anywhere, and win—really win!

I really believe that God is before me, behind me and around me. One thing I know—I never asked to be born. I did not choose my father or mother. I did not choose my race, the color of my skin, or the language that I learned as a child in my family home. I did not choose the community in which I was born and raised. I did not choose the school I attended from the first grade through high school. It was not until college that I made a choice. Even then, there were forces around me which caused me to select my college, and which influenced me to move in certain directions.

One thing I believe, there is a sense of destiny in my life. There is also a sense of destiny about your life. Everything I've said about myself, you could say about yourself. You are God's idea. You are God's dream!

A poet once said that he wished there was some wonderful place called the Land of Beginning Again, where all our cares, heartaches and griefs could be dropped like a shabby old coat at the door and never put on again. Well, there is such a place—the Land of Beginning Again. It is called NOW. In His mercy, God has granted each of us a new beginning at the beginning of each new day. When God is present within us, all things become new!

New beginnings are always open to me for God is with me!

God's Presence

"The Lord will go ahead of you, and he, the God of Israel, will protect you from behind."

Isaiah 52:12

God is with you! He goes before you. He stands behind you! He walks alongside of you. So often, we take His presence with us for granted. Only when difficulties hit and we feel that God has forsaken us, are we conscious of our desire that God be with us.

Today, I want you to think back over the past several weeks or months. Identify an experience in your life where God's presence was clearly seen, if not during the experience, at least His presence was seen in hindsight. Describe that experience:

_____

_____

_____

_____

_____

_____

Now based on that experience, write out an affirmation, like those at the bottom of each page in this book, that will help remind you in the future that God IS present with you, in spite of what the circumstances might appear to say.

_____

_____

God's Presence

"Your godliness will lead you forward, and goodness will be a shield before you, and the glory of the Lord will protect you from behind."

Isaiah 58:8

Isaiah says that the Lord will protect you from behind. God is your rear guard. This comes from a scene of battle. In the Israelite campaigns, in the wilderness and across the promised land, the soldiers always had a vanguard and a rear guard. The vanguard was the scouts that went on ahead to explore the unexplored territory and to suggest a plan to move forward. The rear guard always stayed behind to pick up the pieces and make sure they didn't leave anything valuable behind.

God is our rear guard. I really believe that God is the rear guard in my life. I keep moving along, as you do, sometimes living at too fast a pace, doing things incompletely. But God follows up and finishes what I have done in a half-way measure. I can be confident that God, who has begun a good work in you and me, will complete it.

If you were to take the time to look back, how many tasks would you find uncompleted because the urgency of some new task called you away before you finished? If you have done your best, God will do the rest! I've talked to parents about their teenagers. They say, "If only we had . . ." And I gently remind them they did their best. Now they must trust the rear guard action of God, who finishes the job and picks up the broken pieces, mending them into something wonderful and beautiful. God is that kind of God!

> **Thank you, God, for finishing the tasks I have done imperfectly!**

God's Presence

"I will never, never fail you nor forsake you."

Hebrews 13:5

I have a very dear old friend named Edith, and she has been like a mother to me ever since I have been in California. She is old, very sick, and lives in a rest home. As often as I can I drop in to see her. She hugs me and we kiss each other. I always say to her, "Mom, I will never forget you."

Her eyes brighten and she holds me and says, "Do you mean that, Bob?" And I assure her, "Yes, Mom, I mean it!"

Where are you feeling forsaken today? Briefly describe the situation: _____

_____

_____

Now think of that situation and read again the verse from Hebrews 13:5. If God is with you in that situation where you feel forsaken, what confidence can you have? Describe how God's presence in that situation changes both the situation and you: _____

_____

_____

_____

> In spite of the circumstances and in spite of my feelings I believe God is with me. I can begin to feel His presence! I can feel my attitude beginning to change!

God's Presence

"May the Lord bless and protect you; may the Lord's face radiate with joy because of you; may he be gracious to you, show you his favor, and give you his peace."
Numbers 6:24-26

When Napoleon retreated from Russia, he left the rear guard action in the hands of Marshal Ray. Months passed; the army had all arrived safely in Paris. The battle was over. In the officer's club one night, some were wondering what had happened to the rear guard. One said they were probably wiped out completely. At that moment the door opened and into the room stepped a gaunt, haggard man. Staring blankly from sunken eyes and wearing the tattered uniform of a French general, he just stood there.

"Who are you?" one of the officers finally asked. "I am Marshal Ray." The officers gasped, stood at once and saluted. Then one man ventured the question, "Marshal, where is the rear guard?"

The Marshal dropped his head as he answered, "I am the rear guard. There are no others!"

As Christians we look at the cross and see Jesus Christ. He is our rear guard—there are no others! And in that action He is picking up the pieces, rehabilitating, restoring, filling the voids we left vacant.

If you're carrying an old box full of unnecessary clutter, leave it behind and let God handle it. If you have hurt someone, pray for them, talk with them, and let God heal the hurt. God goes before you, stands behind you and walks with you!

Peace fills my heart and mind for I know that God is with me!

God's Presence

"Let me see your kindness to me in the morning, for I am trusting you. Show me where to walk, for my prayer is sincere."

Psalm 143:8

Arthur Gordon is a favorite writer of mine. Once he came to New York to interview Dr. Blanton, a co-founder of the American Foundation for Religion and Psychiatry. Mr. Gordon sat in a restaurant waiting for the esteemed psychiatrist to arrive. As he waited, his mind went back over his life. By the time Mr. Blanton arrived, Mr. Gordon was sitting there with a frown and a very sad look on his face.

"What's the matter, Arthur?" "Oh," the writer replied, "I've just been sitting here thinking about all the 'ifs' in my life. Dr. Blanton suggested, "Let's drive over to my office after lunch; I want you to hear something."

Later in his office, Dr. Blanton put a tape on a tape recorder and said, "I'm going to let you listen to three different people; they're all patients of mine and they are mentally ill. Listen carefully."

For one hour the great author listened. When the tape was finished, Dr. Blanton asked, "Tell me what single trait all these people had in common." Arthur Gordon thought a moment and then answered, "I can't think of anything."

"Then I'll tell you," the psychiatrist said. "All of them kept repeating the phrase, 'If only . . . if only . . . if only.' Those words cause mental sickness. They are like poison. These people must learn to say, 'Next time . . . next time . . . next time.' These words point to the future, to a new day, to healing and health!"

> **I trust my past to God.**
> **My eyes are on the future!**

God's Presence

"He will make the darkness bright before them and smooth and straighten out the road ahead."

Isaiah 42:16

God is not only the rear guard, but remember, He is the vanguard also—going on ahead of us. As you look into the future you try to imagine what it will be like. Well, I have news for you. God sees problems coming your way of which you are totally unaware. But He will always lead you through those problems, smoothing and straightening out the road ahead of you.

What is a leader? A leader is one at the head of a business, a company, a corporation, an institution or a family. The leader is the one who sees problems that no one else sees and then finds solutions for those problems.

Thus God takes action, quietly, subtly, but strongly; He directs and molds, manipulates and shapes events so that the right solutions become available to you at the right time. He is prepared even before you are aware of the problem. That is the kind of God you and I have—the vanguard moving on ahead.

Some of you look ahead and see little hope because you are imagining your future with God. Don't ever lose sight of Him. He is there constantly ahead of you. Give your life completely to Him. His plan for you is to guide you and lead you. Is there some sin hidden inside of you blocking that vision? Drop it. Do you have a dream? Hold on to it. Is there some goal? Reach for it. God is with you. NOW is the time to move out—today!

God is giving me the courage to move ahead. I can make right decisions because God goes before me and guides!

God's Peace

"I have told you all this so that you will have peace of heart and mind."

John 16:33

Joshua Liebman, in his book titled *Peace of Mind*, tells of an experience he had as a young boy. He made a list of the supreme goods in life and took them to a wise mentor. When he showed him the list, he expected to be praised for his precocity.

The list went something like this . . . "health, love, talent, riches, beauty, faith." As he shared the list with the wise old man, the sage got a twinkle in his eye. He reached for a stub of a pencil and carefully scratched through all of the things Joshua Liebman had listed. Then the old man said, "You man, you may have all of these—health, love, faith, riches, beauty—but they will all turn out to be enemies instead of friends unless you have the one thing you missed." Then he wrote on the paper: "The gift of an untroubled mind."

You may have everything, but if you don't have quietness and peace at the core of your mind, everything else is worthless. Let me share with you the way in which you have peace of mind. I find my wisdom in Jesus Christ. In John 16:33 He said: "I have told you all this so that you will have peace of heart and mind. Here on earth you will have many trials and sorrows; but cheer up, for I have overcome the world."

> **I am serene, calm, undismayed because Jesus Christ gives me His peace!**

God's Peace

" 'Peace! Be still'! And the wind ceased, and there was a great calm."

Mark 4:39 RSV

Jesus talks about peace of heart and mind in the midst of trials and sorrows. How can you reconcile those two thoughts in His statement? Suppose someone had just written you a letter. In that letter, they say, "I thought as a Christian I was supposed to experience peace of mind. But all I experience is chaos, turmoil and anything but peace of mind! What's wrong with me?"

What would you write to them in your return letter?

Write your response here: _I can understand how you feel, but_ _____

_____

_____

_____

_____

_____

_____

_____

_____

**I am centered in Christ!
Nothing can disturb my sense of peace!**

God's Peace

"Turn from all known sin and spend your time in doing good. Try to live in peace with everyone; work hard at it."
Psalm 34:14

I have discovered several principles which, if you apply them to your daily life, will bring you peace of mind. First, enjoy that moment called "Now."

A famous author was raised in Caucasus Mountains. An old hermit lived up in the hills. It was the custom for parents to take their children to visit the old man.

This man's parents took him, along with a gift for the old recluse. In return, he would impart some of his sage wisdom. When they arrived, there were other families waiting. They stayed until it was their turn. Then the young boy walked timidly up to the stern-faced man with the long beard. Reaching out a wrinkled old hand, the gentle man lifted the young boy to his lap, put his arm around him and then waved the other people away.

The young boy handed the sage the little gift he had brought. Taking it, the wise man smiled and asked, "Son, what do you want to do? Where do you want to go? What do you want to be in life?

The lad answered as best he could, and then listened to some wondrous tales of the places the old man had been and what wonderful things he had done in his long, long lifetime. Suddenly he looked the boy straight in the eye and said, "My boy, I want to give you something that will be wonderful while you are young as well as when you are old. Something you can use when you're sad and when you're happy. Here it is; never forget it. This moment, and each moment in life, is part of eternity. Enjoy it!"

> **Now is the most important moment in my life. I enjoy the present!**

God's Peace

"So don't be anxious about tomorrow. God will take care of your tomorrow too. Live one day at a time."

Matthew 6:34

Jesus was always intense about the moment. It is amazing to realize how often we fail to live in the reality of the present moment. We either project ourselves into tomorrow, or fill our thoughts with regret about yesterday.

But think about it. The only thing you can be positive about in life is this present moment. Tomorrow may never come and yesterday is gone forever.

How do you enjoy the moment called "Now?" It's a habit developed through practice. It's a matter of self-discipline in order to enjoy the bird feeding in your backyard, to watch the trees bend in the wind, to linger over the rose growing along the neighbor's fence.

How much time do you spend in the "Now?" Think back over yesterday. How much time did you spend worrying about the future? How much time thinking about the past? How much time enjoying the present moment?

I spent _____% of my time on the future.

I spent _____% of my time on the past.

I spent _____% of my time enjoying the present!

Determine now to live today enjoying the present moments as they unfold. If something about the future comes to mind, make a note. If you remember something of the past, commit it to prayer. Then enjoy to the fullest each moment God gives you!

**I live today as if that is all I have.
God is now!**

God's Peace

Sunshine after rain,
dewdrops on a rose,
a baby sleeping sweetly in the crib,
a bird drinking from a fountain,
a leaf floating on quiet water, and
a mind focused on God.

Such is the peace I feel
deep within my being
now
as
I close my eyes and think about Jesus Christ

Thank you, God.
Amen.

God's Peace

"Agree with God, and be at peace; thereby good will come to you."

Job 22:21 RSV

Peace of mind principle number 2 is to eliminate polyphasic thinking. Now that's a fancy word that simply means the practice of thinking about many things at one time. Many of us have this habit. I got a ticket on the freeway not too long ago due to polyphasic thinking. My mind was occupied with several things, but now with my speed. I paid the penalty!

A leading cardiologist pointed out that polyphasic people are more susceptible to heart disease. His remedy—eliminate the distractions and concentrate on one thing at a time!

The computer is patterned after the mind. Like our brain, it has many channels. We can feed our minds through the eye, the ear, the sense of touch or smell. And each of these channels have many variations. Now if you try to feed information into a computer on more than one channel, you're going to clog up the system.

A computer expert told me that the most glorified, sophisticated, exacting computer made cannot be working on two problems at the same time. It goes crazy.

We can't work on two or more problems at the same time either. Jesus taught the principle that no man can serve two masters. Singleness of mind is the key to peace of mind.

Eliminate polyphasic thinking today! Discipline yourself to think about one thing at a time!

> **My mind is clearly focused on one thing at a time. Today is peaceful because my channels are not clogged!**

God's Peace

"The Lord will give strength unto his people; the Lord will bless his people with peace."

Psalm 29:11 KJV

Let's do some planning to help eliminate polyphasic thinking next week. First make a list of the eight most important things you will need to do next week.

_____

_____

_____

_____

_____

_____

_____

_____

Now go back over your list and number them in order of their importance. The most important task will get number 1, etc. Resolve to concentrate on the most important task during the coming week. When something else comes up go back to work on your priority. Pray that God will give you singleness of mind which leads to peace of mind!

I am calm and peaceful for God is directing my steps!

Peace of Mind

"I will lie down in peace and sleep, for though I am alone, O Lord, you will keep me safe."

Psalm 4:8

Some time back I had the privilege of having lunch with the president of one of the largest aerospace companies. Following lunch, he took me on a tour of his large facility.

What really impressed me was the clean room. My host explained to me that the clean room is so spotless because no particle can pass through the air conditioning system into that room unless it is small enough to fit on the point of a needle. He told me something I didn't know before. The point of a needle is really flat. Put a needle under a microscope and you will see that the point is literally flat. And the largest speck that can come into the clean room will be able to rest on the flat part of the needle point!

To enter that room I had to clear security and then they had to make sure I was clean. It was fascinating, as well as a thought-provoking experience.

You should have a clean room at the center of your life. Your mind should be your own personal clean room. You should have security checks on who and what enters your room. There are some writers I refuse to read because they fill me with negative thoughts, some ideas, some practices that don't pass security. Have you been careless? I suggest you begin today to set up your clean room at the very core of your mind. A place so clean that God is comfortable there. God's dwelling place!

> I am careful about what enters my mind. I think only those thoughts and do those things that foster peace of mind!

Peace of Mind

*"Let us then pursue what makes for peace and for mutual
upbuilding."*

Romans 14:19 RSV

Imagine you have a filter that clears everything entering
your mind. What thoughts, ideas, and practices would be
filtered out? Which would be permitted to enter? Think
carefully about what enters your mind and then make two
lists:

PASSES SECURITY	FILTERED OUT

Spend some time in prayer, talking with God about your
lists. Ask for His help in filtering out all those thoughts,
ideas, and practices that threaten to destroy your peace of
mind. He will!

Today I accept only those thoughts, ideas
and practices which are pleasing to God.
He is with me and gives me peace!

Peace of Mind

"I have told you all this so that you will have peace of heart and mind. Here on earth you will have many trials and sorrows; but cheer up, for I have overcome the world."
                                                            John 16:33

Another principle that leads to peace of mind is to learn to live by the calendar, not by the clock. An enormous amount of inner agitation, emotional disturbance and turbulence, along with disruption of emotional poise and peace comes when we make mountains out of molehills.

Look at a calendar. If you try to think of the year as 365 days, it becomes unmanageable. But when you think of the year as twelve months, already time falls into order. Something else will happen to you. You will start to look at the larger picture.

A great lecturer and writer, Emily Kimbrough, tells about a lesson she once learned. As a little girl ten years old, ready to go on stage for a performance at school, she became very upset because her hair didn't look right. She got frantic—almost hysterical. Her grandmother was with her and said, "Emily, this is nonsense. You would never notice it from a trotting horse."

Emily remembered that advice. Years later she was preparing to lecture to a large audience when she noticed a run in her stocking. For a moment she felt panic; then she remembered Grandma's advice: "Nonsense, Emily, you would never notice it from a trotting horse!"

What you think is so upsetting today is just like trotting by and a year from now nobody will even think about it, not even you. Live by the calendar, not by the clock.

> Lord, help me to major in the majors
> as I live today!

Peace of Mind

"I am leaving you with a gift—peace of mind and heart! And the peace I give isn't fragile like the peace the world gives."

John 14:27

The fifth principle for peace of mind is to make your peace with eternity. Dr. Peale tells of an experience he had as a young boy that shaped his life. He was living in Ohio, where his father, a former medical doctor, was a preacher.

One cold winter night his father received a desperate call to visit someone who was dying. His father hung up the phone, turned to his son and said, "Norman, I think that since you're growing up and fast becoming a young man, you ought to go along with me. They drove to a part of town known as the Red Light district. A crude looking woman was waiting and showed them into the room. There, lying on a bed, was a young woman. The fingers of her child-like hands were spread apart, and lay flat and still on the sheet. She hardly stirred as her breath came in short gasps.

As the older man approached her bed he could see she was very ill. Picking up the girl's tiny hand he looked at her and said, "My girl, you're very sick."

Tears rolled down her face as she said, "Sir, I was raised in a Christian home. How did I ever get here? Oh, will God ever forgive me?" Her small body trembled as she wept, and Norman's father said, "Little lady, do you love Jesus?" She nodded yes. "Can you repeat with sincerity this prayer?" Again, she nodded yes and prayed the sinners prayer. As she said "Amen," the most beautiful peace came over that young girl's face. A moment later she was gone.

> **Old thoughts and old conditions are passed away. I am at peace with God and eternity!**

Peace of Mind

"Therefore, since we are justified by faith, we have peace with God through our Lord Jesus Christ."

Romans 5:1 RSV

Woven throughout this beautiful, peace-generating, love-spreading, power-producing faith we call Christianity is the theme that we have peace with God through our Lord Jesus Christ. St. Paul wrote and told the Romans, "So now, since we have been made right in God's sight by faith in his promises, we can have real peace with him because of what Jesus Christ our Lord has done for us." Jesus said, "The important thing is that your names are registered as citizens of heaven."

There is an eternal consciousness hovering over us. It is an awareness that after this life is over, something else is going to happen. And until we can make peace with eternity, we're just not sure what will happen.

But when we do make peace with eternity, we have peace! Have you made peace with eternity? I know of only one person who can help you do that—Jesus Christ. Only He can forgive your sins. Only He can turn your life around and give you peace. Commit your life to Him today, if you haven't already done so. Then write your commitment below: _____

_____

_____

_____

I commit myself to God.
My heart sings a new song of peace!

Peace of Mind

"Let the peace of heart which comes from Christ be always present in your hearts and lives, for this is your responsibility and privilege as members of his body."

Colossians 3:15

Recently a family came to our church who had just moved to California from New York. They said they couldn't stand another winter in the East shoveling snow. They decided to live the rest of their lives basking in the warm climate of California.

I have a better idea than that. Resolve today to spend the rest of your life basking in the beautiful climate of forgiveness, and be warmed by God's beautiful love. The spirit of forgiveness is the heart of love and leads to genuine peace of mind.

Every so often I spend an evening answering the telephone in our 24 hour telephone counseling center—NEW HOPE. People from all across the country call at all hours to a sympathetic ear and a heart that cares. They simply dial 639-4673. (area code 714). These numbers spell NEW-HOPE.

I picked up a ringing phone and said, "New Hope, may I help you?" The voice on the other end of the line said, "Oh, if you hadn't picked up the phone I would have committed suicide." She went on to unveil a story of jealousy, hatred and resentment toward another woman who loved the same man she loved. Thirty-five minutes later I said, "You have a problem. Your biggest problem is the sin of unforgiveness. You need to forgive and be forgiven." "But how?" she asked. And I had the joy of introducing her to Jesus Christ. As she invited Him into her life, her bitterness and hatred melted away. She discovered the source of peace!

> As I forgive, I walk in peace!

Peace of Mind

"Lord, I need only one thing in this world:
To know myself, and to love God;
Give me, heavenly Father,
your love and your peace.
With these I am rich enough
and desire nothing more;
Sweet and humble heart of Jesus,
make my heart like yours.
Amen

John XXIII

More Than Conquerors

"Overwhelming victory is ours through Christ who loved us enough to die for us."

Romans 8:37

I'm collecting trophies! I hope you are. The trophies I'm trying to win are called the "More Than Conquerors" trophies. Here are some examples of how you can win one.

If you killed an enemy, you are a conqueror; if you turn your enemy into a friend, you are more than a conqueror! If you pull the weeds out of your backyard, you are a conqueror; when you replace the weeds with fruit trees, you are more than a conqueror! When you fight to overcome a hurt and do not strike back in anger at the one who hurt you, you are a conqueror; when you become so strong that troubles do not upset and defeat you, you are a conqueror; when you turn these troubles into productive and fruitful actions, you are more than a conqueror!

In Romans 8, Paul tells us that we can never escape the imperishable love of God; and if we cooperate with God, we can turn our troubles into triumphs. That always wins a "More Than Conqueror" trophy.

Cooperate with God; do not argue and try to coerce Him. There are three simple ways you can turn your troubles into triumphs:

1. Give God thanks—when you face a problem.
2. Give God time—to turn that problem into a triumph.
3. Give God trust—every waiting moment!

God and I are working to turn my troubles into triumphs!

More Than Conquerors

"My Father constantly does good, and I'm following his example."

John 5:17

Carl Sandburg tells the story about Abe Lincoln at the age of seven. One evening, Abe walked over to his cabin door and opened it. He looked up into the face of the full moon and said, "Mr. Moon, what do you see from way up there?"

Mr. Moon answered, "Abe, I see a calendar and it says 1816. I see eight million people in the United States of America. I see 16,000 covered wagons plodding slowly across the midwestern plains toward California. And, Abe, I see far to the west a wagon in the desert between two ridges of the Rocky Mountains. The wagon is broken, weeds are crawling in the spokes and there is an old dusty skeleton nearby with a pair of empty moccasins and some dry bones. I also see a sign that says, "The cowards never started!"

Troubles? Give God thanks! The very fact that you are facing troubles is a compliment to you—you had the courage to stick your neck out and try something. When you have this attitude toward troubles, they generally turn into blessings, compliments, or tributes. When trouble blocks the road and forces you to take a detour which, in turn, spares you from an accident, then trouble becomes a blessing. When suffering forces you to unload excess baggage in your life which you have not had the courage to get rid of before, then trouble is a blessing in disguise! Give God thanks when you face a problem!

> I do not always understand what is happening in my life, but I can thank God always for He is with me!

More Than Conquerors

"God turned into good what was meant for evil."
                                        Genesis 50:20

What problem or trouble are you faced with today?
Describe it briefly: _____

_____

_____

_____

_____

Now, use your imagination and think of all the possible
blessings that could come out of that problem or trouble:

_____

_____

_____

_____

_____

_____

Give God thanks—even as you face trouble!

I let go of anxiety, bitterness and
tension and let God and His goodness
take over my life!

More Than Conquerors

"Day by day the Lord also pours out his steadfast love upon me, and through the night I sing his songs and pray."
Psalm 42:8

Just before Dr. Poppen, one of the most inspiring missionaries I know, returned home from China, the communists had his name tagged. He was earmarked for destruction. After spending forty years in mainland China, devoting his life to Christ's service, he was now a house prisoner.

At the public trial ten thousand people gathered in the city square. Dr. Poppen was paraded on to a platform, falsely accused on many accounts, the most serious being that of treason against the state.

Following the trial, he was led to a tiny prison cell. He could not stand up straight or even lie down straight. There he remained, not knowing what his fate would be. Day after day passed, until that great man of God could take no more. He prayed that God would take him and then fell asleep.

Suddenly he was awakened as the door opened and someone whispered, "Follow me." He was led through a winding, dark cobble-stoned alley until he found himself at the wharf. His companion said, "See that boat? Get on quickly. It will take you to Hong Kong. When you get there, vanish. Good-bye."

As Henry Poppen watched the China mainland disappear, he did not know what lay ahead. He was grateful to God for his freedom and he was thankful that he had given God time to turn his overwhelming problem into triumph! Give God time and you will be more than conqueror!

I am patient. I wait expectantly for God to turn my trouble into triumph!

More Than Conquerors

"Hope in God; for I shall again praise him, my help and my God."

Psalm 42:5 RSV

If I were asked to create a "More Than Conqueror" trophy or banner, I would include the figure of a person standing straight and tall. This person would be holding in one hand a banner upon which would be a shield, on which would be the word, HOPE.

That's my idea. What would you create? Use the space below to either draw a "More Than Conqueror" trophy or banner.

**Today, through Christ,
I am more than conqueror!**

More Than Conquerors

*"And we know that all that happens to us is working for
our good if we love God and are fitting into his plans."*
                                                    Romans 8:28

When I was a young boy, I decided to put my saddle on
a strange horse, pastured on our farm. I rode off heading
for the far reaches of our property. Everything was so
beautiful. I can still see the day—sun shining brightly,
puffy white clouds floating lazily across the Iowa sky, the
temperature just right.

I rode along for some time, when suddenly the horse
became startled at the sight of a tractor. He shied away and
took off at a fast pace. I tugged at the reins, shrieked at him
to stop, kicked his sides furiously—yet nothing even
phased him!

Foaming at the mouth, with nostrils wide and quivering,
and eyes wild with fear, he raced wildly across the gullies
and blindly through the pasture. As he galloped along
crazily, I bounced up and down, back and forth. All I
could do was to hold on to the saddle horn for dear life. I
squeezed my eyes shut and held on until my knuckles
turned white. Unexpectedly, miraculously, the horse
stopped as suddenly as he had begun. I opened my eyes
and there we were in front of the barn door!

If life is taking you on a wild ride, grab hold of the
saddle horn. Take a firm hold, because in life the saddle
horn is a promise of God: "And we know that all that
happens to us is working for our good if we love God and
are fitting into his plans." Give God Trust—every waiting
moment!

I give thanks for my circumstances
because God is working them for my
good! I give thanks in advance!

More Than Conquerors

"We know that to those who love God, who are called according to his plan, everything that happens fits into a pattern for good."

Romans 8:28 Phillips

God knows the future better than I do, therefore I trust Him! Romans 8:28 is a theme verse for my trust. Are you trusting God in the midst of your trouble? Where are you having difficulty trusting Him?

_____

_____

_____

God understands! Write yourself a letter from God about His reaction to your difficulty trusting Him. In your letter, rewrite Romans 8:28, using your difficult situation as an example of one of the things God "fits into a pattern for good."

_____

_____

_____

_____

_____

> **My faith is stronger! I can feel trust welling up within me. I am confident that God can work this out for good!**

God's Prosperity

"My purpose is to give life in all its fullest."

John 10:10

I believe in God's prosperity for my life. In the First Psalm we read that there are people who are so engrafted into God that they are like trees planted by rivers of water, bringing forth fruit every season. They live consistently productive lives! God wants your life to prosper! This week we will look at seven principles of prosperity for your life.

Principle number one: Say something positive about every person and every idea you encounter. There is usually something wrong with every person and idea you meet. Therefore, do not discard a potentially profitable idea simply because there is an objectionable element present. Do not ignore an interesting, helpful person because of some negative quality in their life.

Rather, assume that you can isolate, insulate, and then eliminate or neutralize the negative elements by simply cultivating, exploiting, and capitalizing on the positive elements. Try it: *What is the most negative force in your life today?*_____

Now write down every positive aspect of that force you can think of: _____

_____

_____

_____

> **My attitude is changing. I am looking for the positives and paying less attention to the negatives!**

God's Prosperity

*"The Lord will give you an abundance of good things . . .
just as he promised."*

Deuteronomy 28:11

Principle number two: See something positive every day
in every situation. To achieve success, sell your ideas. Sell
them more zealously if you have a problem. I talked with a
young minister whose ideas for his church were buried
under a mountain of problems, the most pressing of which
was a leaky mimeograph machine! The tight church budget
could include neither a secretary or a new mimeograph.

One afternoon he struggled to print the coming Sunday's
church bulletins. He succeeded only in getting ink stains all
over his clothes and wasted a whole package of paper. In
complete disgust he decided to wear those clothes to the
board meeting that evening.

Several hours later, he was showing the mess to his
board. These men were business men and quickly realized
that they were wasting money and that it would cost even
more money to wait. One man pulled out his wallet and
said, "Reverend, here is $25.00." Another man matched
that, and soon the minister had collected enough for a new
mimeograph machine. He was overcome with joy and dis-
belief. Then he thought to himself, "Possibility thinking
really works!"

Soon, he picked up on some of his other ideas. He
started to "See the positive possibilities in every situation."
He went out visiting, exuberantly urging people to come
to his church. The congregation started growing. His
people saw a more confident minister. Recently they
purchased twenty acres for a new church complex. And it
all started with a leaky mimeograph!

In every situation, I look for the positive!

God's Prosperity

"God is able to provide you with every blessing in abundance, so that you may always have enough of everything and may provide in abundance for every good work."

2 Corinthians 9:8 RSV

Principle number three: Develop the daily habit of always thinking "It might work." A maid named Matilda did this. Her employer, a wealthy woman, was concerned when she learned that Matilda had no savings for the future. She said, "Matilda, suppose we lose our investments; suppose I have to let you go; then suppose you cannot find new work; suppose you do not have an income? What are you going to do?"

Matilda replied, "That is all you do . . . suppose, suppose, suppose. There is no suppose in my Bible; there is only repose. My Bible says, 'Surely goodness and mercy shall follow me all the days of my life.' "

We get caught up in the "suppose it won't work" syndrome. It's time to change that to "It might work!" Where in your life do you need to start affirming, "It might work!"? Take what appears to be an impossible situation that you are facing this week and think of four ways that it just might possibly work:

1. _____

2. _____

3. _____

4. _____

> God wants me to prosper. Whatever I touch, in faith, will work out!

God's Prosperity

"Light is sown for the godly and joy for the good."
                                                    Psalm 97:11

Principle number four: Appoint yourself president of your own "Why Not" club. Ed is a brilliant young lawyer who recently moved to California. He and his wife, Pat, have no relatives out here, and as Thanksgiving drew near, they realized they were alone. But they also realized that hundreds of old people in the area were forsaken and lonely. So they decided to found a "Why Not" club. Ed was president and Pat was vice-president.

They decided to have a Thanksgiving dinner for those lonely forgotten people. Ed went to one of the local hotels and asked if there was a big, empty convention banquet hall available for Thanksgiving. He explained his plan to the manager, but received a very curt "No." Undaunted, Ed asked, "Why not?" The manager was taken back, thought a moment and then agreed, "All right!"

Then Ed went to some of the companies his law firm dealt with and asked them for money for the dinner. He knew they had money for charities, but received the expected, "No, we have a policy about our donations. Your plan doesn't meet our policy." "Why not?" Ed asked. Again, he was successful and raised the necessary funds. They made all the arrangements and then waited for Thanksgiving noon to arrive.

At 11:40, the first guest arrived—a little old lady. By noon over 300 people shared the spirit of Thanksgiving because Ed and Pat asked the question, "Why not?"

If someone else can succeed and prosper, *Why not* you?

> I am ready for the success and
> prosperity God has for me!

God's Prosperity

*"Out of his glorious, unlimited resources he will give you
the mighty inner strengthening of His Holy Spirit."*
                                          Ephesians 3:16

Prosperity principle number five: Honor every positive
idea that comes into your mind with the D.I.N. degree.
When positive ideas come into my mind, I write them
down on paper immediately. I think this is important,
especially if you want to prosper—write it down. Then,
in front of every good idea, write D.I.N. That means Do It
Now!

Sir Alexander Fleming, a Scottish bacteriologist,
discovered the life-saving antibiotic, Penicillin. One
morning in his laboratory, he observed that the fungus
around the bacteria on a culture plate had died. He took a
bit of the mold and put it in an empty glass tube for further
study. The result—penicillin. Sir Alexander observed
something interesting and he did something about it
immediately. He was definitely a person who believed in
honoring an intriguing idea with the D.I.N. degree.

What could you do today about one of your positive
ideas? What important step could you honor with the
D.I.N. degree? Describe the step you will take today:

_____

_____

_____

_____

> I lack nothing. I thank God for my
> prosperity as I act on His ideas
> and His riches!

God's Prosperity

"The blessing of the Lord makes rich."

Proverbs 10:22 RSV

Prosperity principle number six: practice the principle of positive expectations. Why do some people always seem to prosper? Because they expect to prosper.

Several years ago, a minister and a group of his congregation decided at year's end to test the power of expectations. Each person wrote down his New Year's expectations, put them into an envelope, sealed them, and then agreed to meet and read them aloud at the same time the following year. The results were fascinating.

One man wrote, "In the next year all I can expect is more of the same old miserable life." What do you think he got? A woman in the group listed ten worthy goals she expected to achieve. Nine of them had been accomplished by the time they met again. She admitted that because she expected to reach these goals, she really worked hard at them.

Another man wrote, "As none of the men in my family have survived beyond the age of sixty, I expect I may die this year." He died one month before his sixtieth birthday! Each person in the group was surprised to see that everyone got almost exactly what they expected.

Expect prosperity! Open yourself to new ideas, knowing that your energy, your resources, your supply comes from God's bountiful storehouse of riches. You have infinite resources and therefore you have infinite possibilities. EXPECT PROSPERITY! EXPECT THE BEST! You will get what you expect.

**I am prospered by God's rich resources.
I expect prosperity!**

God's Prosperity

"I will open up the windows of heaven for you and pour out a blessing so great you won't have room enough to take it in."

Malachi 3:10

Prosperity principle number seven: Discipline yourself to become a positive reactionary. Dr. Peale was once asked how far he would go in applying Positive Thinking. He replied, "I apply it to all situations over which I have control," I agree!

Occasions will arise in your life over which you have no control. Suppose a loved one was killed in an automobile accident. You had no control over this tragic mishap. BUT you can control your reaction! What will you do? What will this event do to you? Misfortune never leaves you where it found you. It either changes you, or you change a negative event into a positive force for good. Become a positive reactionary. Use you head. Make the best of every situation. React positively!

J. Wallace Hamilton talked about being in the desert between the Arab and Israeli sections one time when the fighting was heavy. He saw a small boy playing on a flute and said, "Come here, lad." As the boy approached him, he noticed that the flute was made from a rifle barrel. An instrument of destruction had been turned into an instrument for making beautiful music. That's being a positive reactionary. That is turning obstacles into opportunities.

Right now, the Spirit of God is working within you to open up new opportunities. Prayer puts you in tune with God's ideas and attitudes. Open yourself to His abundant prosperity!

> **God's spirit is changing my attitudes.
> I am a positive reactionary!**

Prayer Is The Key

"And when you draw close to God, God will draw close to you."

James 4:8

I believe in prayer. It is the communion of my heart with the heart of the eternal. Prayer has the power to do several things in my life. Today, I want you to focus on the *draining* power of prayer. This is a power that enables you to drain the negative emotion out of your life.

If you want to have the abundant life that Jesus Christ came to offer you, it is necessary to drain negative emotions out of your soul—fear, suspicion, distrust, hate, resentment, jealousy, insecurity, self-pity. Jesus Christ has the power to drain these defeatist feelings from your life. In their place, He will fill you with positive ideas—love, courage, hope, good humor, cheer, optimism, enthusiasm, self-confidence.

I experienced a conflict with a person who is a real terrible trouble-maker. He destroyed his wife's life; he destroyed his son's life; he destroyed the lives of many people. I tried to help him and he turned on me. It was a terrifying experience. I woke up in the middle of the night, and my heart was filled with negative feelings toward him. I thought, it is not right for me to have such negative attitudes toward another person. I am a Christian; I am a follower of Christ.

As I lay in bed, I prayed that God would drain out of me all those negative feelings. I imagined myself as a car up on the grease rack with the mechanic underneath, removing the plug and letting all the dirty old oil pour out of the crankcase. And that is exactly what Christ did with my attitude toward this man. It was a miracle!

**Prayer is a miracle!
As I pray, God works!**

Prayer Is The Key

"I love the Lord because He hears my prayers and answers them. Because he bends down and listens, I will pray as long as I breathe!"

Psalm 116:1, 2

Ruth Carter Stapleton tells of an experience in prayer. "When my daughter started the first grade, she began to have terrible pains. Up to that time, I loved my little girl so much I never let her out of my sight. I didn't realize then that it was my insecurity that caused me to be so over-protective. So when she started school, without my constant attention, she became sick. I took her to several doctors and they all said it wasn't a physical problem, so I took her to a psychiatrist.

" 'This child has deep emotional problems', the doctor said. 'She will need therapy four days a week for a long time. We'll put her on the waiting list and call you.'

"I was devasted My child was emotionally ill and I was the one responsible for her problems. I took my little girl home and every night after she went to bed, I would pray over her. I waited to make sure everybody was asleep because I wasn't sure God would answer my prayers. Each night I would pray, 'Lord Jesus, bridge the gap between the love she needed and the love she got.' I never missed a night!

"Seven months later, the clinic called and said I could bring her in to begin therapy. I took her immediately and they ran tests for two days. To the amazement of everyone, myself included, the results of those tests showed my daughter perfectly normal.

"Jesus reached back into the past as I prayed, and filled the empty places. That was the beginning of my prayer life!"

Through prayer, Jesus is changing me!

Prayer Is The Key

*"Search me, O God, and know my heart; test my
thoughts. Point out anything you find in me that makes
you sad, and lead me along the path of everlasting life."*
                                        Psalm 139:23, 24

I received a letter I want to share with you. Here is what
the letter said: "Two months ago I did not believe in God.
I tried to commit suicide four times. I hated God. My life
was nothing and I didn't care. No one could help; not the
doctors or my husband! Then one Sunday my husband
forced me to listen to the Hour of Power. Rev. Schuller,
you were talking about making your enemies into your
friends. I began to think.

"I had not spoken to my parents for years. I hated them
for putting me into a foster home as a child. They had tried
to contact me, but I never answered. They were on top of
my enemy list!

"As I thought about them as enemies, I decided it was
time to make them friends. I asked Don to take me to see
them and when we arrived, I thought they would have a
heart attack. But we talked, and I forgave them. I think
that evening was the nicest time I had ever had in my life.
Since then, all the anger and bitterness has drained away.
Jesus does make a difference!"

As you pray and allow all the negative feelings to drain
out of your life, is there someone you need to call or write?
Why not sit down now and turn an enemy into a friend.
It's all part of God's draining system!

> I allow God to drain away all negative
> feelings. All my relationships are an
> expression of God's healing power!

Prayer Is The Key

"We can be mirrors that brightly reflect the glory of the Lord. And as the Spirit of the Lord works within us, we become more and more like Him.

2 Corinthians 3:18

A well known Indian from New Delhi, Sulwit Shoorar, was converted to Christianity. After his conversion, he let his hair grows in curls on his shoulders, dressed in a white tunic with a gold rope vest, and wore sandals on his tanned feet.

He was asked to come to America for a speaking tour through various Christian churches. Upon his acceptance, he was given the address of a minister in New York City. Shoorar put the address in safekeeping.

When he reached New York, he gave the slip of paper to a taxi driver. The taxi drove to the address and stopped, Shoorar paid the fare, stepped out, went to the door of the house, and rang the bell.

The minister's small son opened the door and stared wide-eyed at the tall man, dressed in a white robe, with long brown hair and large, dark, warm eyes. Looking down at the little boy, the man from India said, "My name is Sulwit Shoorar. Is your father home?"

The boy stammered, "J-J-Just a minute." He ran into the house and told his father there was someone at the front door to see him. His father asked, "Who is it; what is his name?" "I can't remember what he said, Daddy," the boy answered, "but he sure looks like Jesus."

Prayer gives me *gaining* power—the ability to gain more and more the attitude and mind of Jesus Christ.

Jesus is the hero of my soul. I love to talk with Him in prayer!

Prayer Is The Key

"Cast your burden on the Lord, and He will sustain you."
Psalm 55:22 RSV

Prayer gives you draining power, gaining power, and prayer also gives you *sustaining* power! Sustaining power is the power to hold on and never quit in life.

One of my favorite inspirational sayings was found scratched on the wall of a basement in Germany after World War II. Some nameless Jew in hiding had scratched the Star of David on the wall along with the following statement.

I believe in the sun even when it is not shining.

I believe in love even when I do not feel it.

I believe in God even when He is silent.

That's a power-filled faith. That kind of faith can only come to the person who knows the sustaining power of prayer. When all is darkness, this person is still basking in the warm sunlight of God's presence through prayer.

If you were trapped in some dark basement somewhere, what could you scratch on the wall? Write you own trilogy of faith:

I believe in _____

I believe in _____

I believe in _____

Amen!

I sing to the Lord because
He gives me sustaining power!

Prayer Is The Key

*"May my spoken words and unspoken thoughts be
pleasing even to you, O Lord my Rock and my Redeemer."*
                                              Psalm 19:14

The president of one of the country's largest steel
companies learned an important lesson one day. A man
came to see him and said, "Sir, I know you have many
advisors, but give me five minutes. If what I say is
unimportant, you owe me nothing. If I have helped you,
your company may send me a check for whatever amount
you think this advice is worth."

The chief executive brusquely said, "All right, you have
five minutes." The man said, "Here is a piece of paper. List
the important things you have to do today. Now, please
number the items according to priority of importance."
The company president did as he was instructed.

"Now," continued the visitor, "begin with item number
one and do not work on anything else until item number
one is completed. Then go on to item number two and do
the same thing. If you follow this procedure, and have
your executives do the same, your company will improve
in its management, organization and profit." Six months
later, the man received a check for $25,000.

Why not do the same thing with your prayers? Make a
list of the most important things you can pray for. Then
number them according to priority and pray faithfully for
item number one. You will want to pray for other things
on your list, but make it a point to pray for item number
one everytime you pray. Then be ready—God is up to
something great!

**The power of prayer is enhancing my
life and the lives of others!**

Prayer Is The Key

The Lord has a job for me,
But I had so much to do;
I said, "You find somebody else, Lord,
Or wait 'til I get through."
I don't know how the Lord made out;
But He seemed to get along.
Yet, I felt a kind of sneaking
Like I had done the Good Lord wrong.

One day I needed the Lord,
Needed Him right away;
But He never answered me at all.
And I could hear Him say
Down in my accusing heart,
"Black man, I has got too much to do;
Yet get somebody else
Or wait 'til I get through."

Now when the Lord's got a job for me.
I never tries to shirk;
I drops whatever I has got on hand
And I does the Good Lord's work.
And my affairs can run along
Or wait 'til I get through;
Nobody else can do the job
That God has planned for you.

Paul Lawrence Dunbar

Abundant Living

"He has told you what He wants, and this is all it is: to be fair and just and merciful and to walk humbly with your God."

Micah 6:8

One of my very dear friends, Dione Neutra, was for over forty years the faithful, adoring wife of the internationally famed architect, Richard Neutra, who was also the architect of our present church sanctuary. Richard died a few years ago, and Dione surprised everybody by developing a tremendous, dynamic life on her own. She frequently writes to us.

In a recent letter she wrote, "You know, people are astounded at my vitality. They tell me that I am an inspiration to them. I can't understand it. Some say I don't get any older at all; but I look in the mirror and I know that is not true.

"I am amazed. How can I be an inspiration to people? Richard was always the inspirator. How is it possible that now I can be the inspirator? I am getting old. What is true is that I have a great zest for life. My life has always had a purpose. I always have a task to fulfill. I have enjoyed what I have had to do. If I have not enjoyed it, I have been able to recognize that whatever was disagreeable to me was also a fact of life. I had to be patient and persevere. It's a mystery how I can be an inspiration.

"The other day I met a woman who was completely lost when her husband died. She did not know what to do with her life; whereas I know exactly what I want to do with the remaining years of my life. Perhaps that is my secret!" Abundant living begins with living for a purpose!

> **I abide in God's abundance.**
> **I know why I am alive.**

Abundant Living

"For to me, living means opportunities for Christ."
Philippians 1:21

People often ask me, "How can I know God's will for my life?" And I usually answer by saying, "That's the wrong question. The right question to be asking is 'How can I accomplish God's plan for me?' "

You see, God's will for you is clear. He wills that you be born again. That's basic. God wants you to experience the new birth. Secondly, God wants you to succeed. He has promised to "crown your efforts with success!" (Proverbs 3:6). Thirdly, God wants you to serve Him, His will is that simple.

The big question is "How will you accomplish His plan?" And the key to the correct answer to that question is to identify your purpose in life. What is your purpose for living? Briefly describe it : _____

_____

_____

_____

I define the purpose of a Christian like this: A mind through which Christ thinks, a heart through which Christ loves, a voice through which Christ speaks; a hand through which Christ lifts, and a soul through which Christ glows. That's Abundant Living!

> Lord, today make me an
> instrument of Your peace!

Abundant Living

"Oh, that we might know the Lord! Let us press on to know Him, and He will respond to us as surely as the coming of dawn or the rain of early spring."

Hosea 6:3

One of the saddest sights in life today is to see someone buy into the empty promises of the world. It reminds me of the story told by Dr. Clovus Shapel, one of the great ministers of the South. He says, "I remember when I was a boy attending Sunday School. One Christmastime our Sunday school class had a party. What a surprise! There was a Christmas tree with presents, and even a Santa to give out the presents. One by one we would go up and get our gifts. It was beautiful.

"Included among our group was a boy who was six inches taller than the rest of us. He was the village idiot. He sat there with his mouth open and his eyes staring, eagerly waiting for his name to be called. Gift after gift was passed out until they were almost gone. The boy was getting discouraged and was about to burst into tears.

"At that moment, Santa went behind the tree, pulled out a big gift, and read off the boy's name. A look of joy spread over his face as he grabbed the package, ripped off the wrapping and opened the box. And then despair replaced his joy. Somebody had decided to play a joke on the lad and the box was empty. The boy shook the box, then walked out of the room, his head drooping, shoulders bowed and tears pouring down his face. I'll never forget that sight!"

You say, "What a dirty trick!" Agreed! But the world plays the same trick on you and me when it promises and doesn't deliver. Only Jesus Christ can give Abundant Life!

> **My abundance comes from God!**

Abundant Living

*"Set your heart on His kingdom and His goodness, and all
these things will come to you as a matter of course."*
                                        Matthew 6:33 Phillips

Society comes to you with beautiful packages that are
really empty. Madison Avenue offers money, fame, or
youth and they present these empty gifts as the beautiful
source of real satisfaction. But these gifts do not satisfy.

Yet everyday we see empty promises on billboards, television and magazine ads. Identify some of these
promises—perhaps the ones that are most tempting
to you: _____

_____

_____

_____

_____

_____

Now look again at the verse in Matthew 6:33. Rewrite it
in your own words, relating it to Madison Avenue's
promises: _____

_____

_____

_____

> **God's kingdom comes first in my life!**

Abundant Living

"Always full of the joy of the Lord, and always thankful to the Father who has made us fit to share all the wonderful things that belong to those who live in the kinddom of light."

Colossians 1:11, 12

Whenever I am tempted to go out and buy the latest appliance, I am reminded of Dan Crawford, the man who replaced Dr. Livingston in Africa. Crawford spent twenty-eight years serving that area.

Along about his twenty-second year, Crawford thought about going home. He told a Bantu chief, "I have been here a long time. I think I will go home." The chief replied, "Where is home?" "England," Crawford answered.

Then he sat down and told his black Christian brother what England was like. He described the ships that sailed on the seas. He told him about the long trains with the locomotives that billowed out great puffs of smoke. He related the beauty of the huge bridges made of steel spanning the great rivers of his homeland.

Crawford continued, "The homes have a knob you turn and running water comes out of a pipe, right in the house. You can wash or take a bath. You can even go to a wall, push a button and light will come on in the room."

As Crawford became lost in his memories, the old chief interrupted, "Is that all?" Crawford was silent. Finally the chief said, "But, to be better off is not to be better!"

In fact, today, it might even be worse. Yet all of our materialism comes into the right perspective when Jesus Christ is at the center of our lives. Abundant living is not made up of things!

I give thanks for this progressive world. But my life centers on God and His abundance!

Abundant Living

"Yes, happy are those whose God is Jehovah."

Psalm 144:15

What gives you the most satisfaction in life? When the crowds are gone, the picnic baskets are empty and the air is silent, what really satisfies? Think for a moment and then make a list: _____

_____

_____

_____

_____

_____

Now read again Psalm 144:12-15. Let's write our own ending to that great Psalm. Here's the beginning, you do the rest:

"Here is my description of a truly happy place . . .

_____

_____

_____

_____

_____

> **I sing a song of thanksgiving!**

Abundant Living

"For the man who uses well what he is given shall be given more, and he shall have abundance."

Matthew 25:29

E. Stanley Jones makes a point about the condition upon which God's guarantee of abundance is made. All of God's promises are conditional, for God must not merely give— He must give in such a way that the person receiving is stimulated, not smothered. God must not merely make a gift; He must make a person.

Abundant living does not come through constantly receiving. Abundant living depends upon abundant giving. Everyone should receive according to need, but everyone must also give according to ability. Frank Laubach puts it this way: "The human organism is a sprinkler head. By itself, a sprinkler head is not worth very much, but attach it to a hose, let the water flow through, and the sprinkler head makes flowers grow, turns grass green and creates parks where children can play.

"Your life, in God's plan, is to be a sprinkler head for Jesus Christ." Jesus said, "Out of you shall flow rivers of living water." This is God's purpose that satisfies. I admit, by comparison, all the other purposes which appear as beautiful gifts given to you by society and culture are empty promises. The only purpose that satisfies is Jesus Christ!

> I feel a growing generosity within me.
> I want to share all that God
> has given to me!

Forgiveness

"... and forgive us our sins, just as we have forgiven those who have sinned against us."

Matthew 6:12

"Your heavenly Father will forgive you if you forgive those who sin against you ..."

Matthew 6:15

"When you are praying, first forgive anyone you are holding a grudge against, so that your Father in heaven will forgive you your sins too."

Mark 11:25

"Father, forgive these people," Jesus said, "for they don't know what they are doing."

Luke 23:34

"I bless the holy name of God with all my heart. Yes, I will bless the Lord and not forget the glorious things he does for me. He forgives all my sins."

Psalms 103:1-3

Forgiveness

". . . we see God's abounding grace forgiving us."
                                              Romans 5:20

An esteemed English clergyman told J. Wallace Hamilton, "The turning point came in my life when I was 17 years old. I always had trouble with my brothers and sisters. I was called the black sheep in the family. We were always fighting each other.

"One night they were all picking on me until I could stand it no longer. I jumped up and cried, 'I'm getting out of here!' I ran up the stairs and there suddenly in the darkened hallway I ran into my grandmother. She had been listening to it all. She stood there in the hallway and stopped me by putting her hand on my shoulder. With tears in her eyes she said only a few words to me, but they changed my life. She said, *'John, I believe in you.'* "

And right now, can't you see Jesus? He comes down from the cross and stops you in the middle of your tracks by putting His nail-scarred hand on your shoulder. He says to you, "I've heard everything, and I want you to know, *I believe in you!*"

What a great moment that is! And when, you've experienced His acceptance and forgiveness, you'll become a forgiving person yourself!

> **God, you believe in me!**
> **Thank You for that thought.**

Forgiveness

"God can be depended on to forgive us . . ."

1 John 1:9

Write God a "Thank you note" for His gift of forgiveness:

Dear God: _____

_____

_____

_____

_____

_____

_____

_____

_____

_____

_____

God has forgiven me, is forgiving me, and He will forgive me!

Forgiveness

"But we Christians . . . can be mirrors that brightly reflect the glory of the Lord. And as the Spirit of the Lord works within us, we become more and more like him."
2 Corinthians 3:18

Legend tells us that the beautiful Helen of Troy, over whom many battles were fought, was lost after one of the battles. When the army returned to Greece, Helen was not on any of the ships. Menelaus went to try and find her, at great personal peril. He finally found her in one of the seaport villages. She had been suffering from amnesia. Forgetting who she was, she had stooped to the lowest possible level and was living as a prostitute.

Menelaus found her in rags, dirt, shame, and dishonor. He looked at her and called, "Helen." Her head turned. "You are Helen of Troy!" he said. And with those words, her back straightened and the royal look came back. She had been redeemed!

You may be deflated and dishonored in your own eyes because you don't realize who you are. You are a member of the royal family. When you accept Jesus Christ into your life, you are a member of the family of God. You are no longer a lost soul. You have been forgiven and have recovered your honor!

I am a member of Christ's family!

Forgiveness

"Now it is the time to forgive."

2 Corinthians 2:7

My Forgiveness List

I find it very hard to forgive _____

for _____

Because God has forgiven me, I want to forgive _____

_____ . I will let _____ know by

_____ and saying _____

_____

_____

_____

_____

_____

> **With God's ability,
> I am a forgiving person!**

Forgiveness

"He who forgives an offense seeks love."
Proverbs 17:9 RSV

Express your joy in forgiveness by creating a special forgiveness poem. This is a poetry form that is easy enough that anyone can do it. The first line is one word—the title. Line two has two words which describe the title. Line three is three words long and contains action words or phrases about the title. Line four has four words that describe your feelings about the title. And line five is one word that restates the title. For example:

> Forgiveness
> God's Gift
> Sets me free
> So glad it's possible
> Grace

_____

_____   _____

_____   _____   _____

_____   _____   _____

_____

> The more I forgive, the more love I experience. Thank you, Lord, for Your forgiveness.

Forgiveness

"Lord, if you keep in mind our sins then who can ever get an answer to his prayers? But you forgive! What an awesome thing this is!"

Psalm 130:4

During the first World War, the German armies swept over Belgium, destroying many of the cities. One day after the war was over, a Catholic nun with a group of her little students paused at a small Catholic shrine at the edge of the village. They knelt in prayer and began to repeat the Lord's Prayer. But they couldn't utter one phrase.

Around them was the rubble and the ruin, the resentment and the hurt of the war years. The small group started again, "Forgive us our trespasses as we . . ." They could go no further— until from behind them came a strong man's voice—"As we forgive those who trespass against us." They looked around and saw King Albert! With his great spirit of forgiveness, he led the way!

Christ, our King, shows us how to conquer resentment and hurt. It was our King who cried from the cross, "Father, forgive them, for they know not what they do."

Perhaps you need to forgive someone. Ask your King— Jesus Christ—to give you the ability. God can help you be a forgiving person. And He will flood your being with love, peace and joy!

> You, Lord, are helping me now to forgive others as You have forgiven me.

God Is Able!

"Now glory be to God who by his mighty power at work within us is able to do far more than we would ever dare to ask or even dream of—infinitely beyond our highest prayers, desires, thoughts, or hopes."

Ephesians 3:20

What do you do when you reach the spot where the burdens of life become just too heavy and are more than you can bear? How do you "get hold of yourself" when your whole world seems to be falling apart at your feet? Where do you turn when there are no answers and you're tempted to blurt out those nasty words, "—but there's no way?"

Here is the answer: Remember that God is ABLE! When you don't know how to handle the burdens of life, God is able! The Christian faith offers hope. And that hope is based on the power of God!

Do you feel weighted down by something today? Perhaps it is a burden within your own life, or a problem that is caused by someone else—a relative, neighbor or associate at work. Now use possibility thinking and list several ways in which God could possibly lift your burden.

_____

_____

Now read again Ephesians 3:20 and dare to ask God for an answer. God is able!

> **The joy of the Lord strengthens me. I am excited because God is working in my life.**

God Is Able!

"For God has not given us the spirit of fear; but of power."
2 Timothy 1:7 KJV

When you focus your whole attention, thought, time and heart upon the person and character of Jesus Christ, believe me—things change!

As a small boy growing up on our Iowa farm, I had very few toys. Those were the depression years and the dust bowl years. What few toys we did have were either hand-made or were treasured items salvaged from some junk pile. One of my most treasured toys was an old chipped piece of a magnifying glass. I used to sit in my overalls by the river bank, and when the fish weren't biting, I would take this piece of a magnifying glass and focus the sun's rays on the ground. I would sit for hours fascinated by the little round, hot, yellow spots on the dry glass that would begin to curl into smoke.

The secret was to get the power of the sun's rays into focus. The same is true of God's Son. When you focus the power of the Son of God upon your heart, a fire is going to kindle deep within you, I assure you. A flame of faith will flash within you!

Lord, You are focusing Your power into my life. I feel stronger. My faith is growing.

God Is Able!

"But you shall receive power when the Holy Spirit has come upon you."

Acts 1:8 RSV

Can you imagine how those first disciples felt as they walked down from the mountain? What excitement! Jesus had just told them they would receive power! But wait—the words of Jesus are true today. Jesus is looking at you and saying; "YOU shall receive power . . . !"

As you listen to Him, what goes through your mind? Where would you like God's power focused in your life? Write it down:

_____

_____

_____

_____

_____

_____

_____

Jesus made a promise. He always keeps His promises! God is able and His power is available for you today.

> **The power of God is at work in my life today. I am able because God is able!**

God Is Able!

"My health fails; my spirits droop, yet God remains! He is the strength of my heart; he is mine forever!"

Psalm 73:26

I have been inspired by the story of George Smith, the Moravian missionary. All of his life he wanted to be a missionary to Africa. Everything he did was directed towards that goal.

He finally finished his preparation and set sail for Africa. His lifelong dream and calling was now a reality. But he was in Africa only a few months when the government expelled him from the land. When he was expelled he left behind only one convert—an old woman. He was still a young man when he died. He died on his knees praying for Africa; for the people he had come to love.

Think of it! All of his life was spent in preparation. He prepared for a ministry of only a few months and then died a young man. But one hundred years later, the seed planted in the life of one old woman had multiplied into 13,000 happy African Christians!

Anyone can look at the externals—anyone can count the seeds in an apple. But only God can count the apples in a seed! Only God knows the end from the beginning. God is able! You are able as you possibilitize through your faith and multiply what God is going to do!

**I anchor myself in God and
I feel secure and strong.**

God Is Able!

"He who hears the word and understands it; he indeed bears fruit, and yields, in one case a hundredfold, in another sixty, and in another thirty."

Matthew 13:23 RSV

The parable of the sower gives several important insights on how you can have a multiplying faith.

First, it is important to listen with an expectant attitude to the word of God. Jesus said, "But with God, everything is possible." (Matthew 19:26).

Second, the sower must sow the seed. He must *act as if it is possible.* He must go out into the field and work. Now this means that you must act-as-if-you-believed that "With God, everything is possible!" How?

Look back at what you wrote down on Tuesday. Where do you want God's power focused in your life? Describe how you would live and act IF God's power was focused in at that point of your life:

_____

_____

_____

_____

_____

Lord, You are helping me to live as-if-I-believed that with You, everything is possible! I really believe it is possible!

God Is *Able!*

"He is able to save completely all who come to God through him."

Hebrews 7:25

Several years ago I was traveling through Russia. While going through the Museum of Atheism in Luvov, I prayed that God would allow me to say something to our young Communist guide.

As the tour ended, I looked at her and said, "Before I say good-bye, I have good news for you." "What's that?" she asked. And I answered, watching her eyes very carefully for any reaction, "God loves you, even if you don't believe in Him. You may be an atheist. You have that freedom— you have that right. But that doesn't change God one bit. He still loves you even if you don't believe in Him." And then she winced.

To this day I have felt that was one of those sacred times in my life when an off-the-cuff comment was prompted by God's Holy Spirit. I believe that Spirit-directed comment powerfully burned its way into a consciousness and will never leave that girl's mind! I dare to believe with all my being that she was cybernetically tattooed with that concept. I have no doubt in my mind that someday she will become a believer!

When God's Holy Spirit prompts you to do or say something, pay attention. That powerful thought or action can be used by God to bring about seemingly impossible changes! God is able!

> **Today, I am sensitive to the special moments the Holy Spirit is preparing for me.**

God Is Able!

It is flowing into me now,
for my conscience is clear.
I have made the right decision.
I am not afraid of problems.
I will face changes calmly and serenely
for
God is behind me.
He will help me.
If I must go through difficult times,
he will rescue me.
I feel His spirit of confidence surging in
my heart now.

With Him I cannot possibly fail.
"If God is for me who can be against me?"
I have a strong feeling
that
everything is going to work out just beautifully.

Thank you, God.
Amen.

God Cares!

"Blessed are those who mourn, for they shall be comforted."

Matthew 5:4 RSV

As a pastor, I am in the specialized work of dealing with the hurt, the lonely, the suffering, the sick and the dying. For over twenty years I have trudged the soft, green lawns of cemeteries with my arms around wives, husbands, fathers, mothers, relatives and friends. I have sat in hospitals and wept with those who were weeping. Believe me, I am not blind to the reality of suffering.

William Saroyan recently said in a television interview, "Sorrow is a cloud which hangs over everyone, always in this life." None of us escapes the very human pain and heartache that comes when we or someone close to us suffers.

But, I have good news! Jesus said it: "Blessed are those who mourn, for they shall be comforted!" In the words of the old hymn, "Earth has no sorrow that heaven cannot heal."

It is possible for the vacant spot to be filled with a new love. It is possible for the smashed vase to be tenderly repaired and restored, or replaced. It is possible to make a comeback after heartbreak. It is possible because GOD CARES!

> **Surely the Lord is in my sorrow and pain and I believe God cares!**

God Cares!

"Blessed is the man who endures trial."

James 1:12 RSV

Too many of us will simply not slow down long enough to hear God's voice until we enter the valley of suffering. If your suffering turns you to God, does it not become a blessing?

The prophet Isaiah wrote, "The year King Uzziah died I saw the Lord!" (Isaiah 6:1). Many a father and mother have been converted to Christ through the death of a child. But what good is that to the child, the cynic asks. Jesus Christ answered that question when He said, "Except a grain of wheat fall into the ground and die . . . it bears no fruit." (John 12:24 KJV). "He who believes in Me shall live even if he dies." (John 11:25 NASB).

There is no birth without birth pangs. And there is no entrance into eternal life except through the birth experience the world calls death.

Are you facing trials or troubles? Rejoice for God is illuminating your path. He is conditioning you for a life of more effective service. *In love's service only broken hearts will do!*

_____

_____

_____

I am turning my sorrow into my servant and I am a better servant than before.

God Cares!

Count your garden by the flowers;
Never by the leaves that fall.
Count your days by golden hours;
Don't remember clouds at all.
Count your nights by stars, not shadows;

Count your life with smiles, not tears.
And with joy on every birthday,
Count your age by friends, not years!

"Be glad for all God is planning for you.
Be patient in trouble, and prayerful
always."   Romans 12:12

God Cares!

"Take your share of suffering as a good soldier of Jesus Christ."

2 Timothy 2:3

John Wesley was once talking with a farmer friend. Wesley noticed a cow with its head over a stone wall and was perplexed. He asked the farmer, "Why would that cow be trying to look over the wall?" The farmer answered, "Well, that's simple. She's looking over the wall because she can't see through it."

Life is full of problems, setbacks, rejections, disappointments, discouragements. Even your prayers may seemingly go unanswered. You reach a point where you think God has forsaken you—prayer is ineffective and God no longer seems real. You've run into a stone wall!

What do you do when you run into a stone wall and feel you just can't cope anymore? You stand there patiently and look over the stone wall. "We can rejoice, too, when we run into problems and trials for we know that they are good for us—they help us learn to be patient. And patience develops strength of character in us and helps us trust God more each time we use it until finally our hope and faith are strong and steady. Then, when that happens, we are able to hold our heads high no matter what happens and know that all is well, for we know how dearly God loves us, and we feel this warm love everywhere within us because God has given us the Holy Spirit to fill our hearts with his love." (Romans 5:3-5).

> I am able to rejoice in my sufferings because God is working in my life.

God Cares!

"When you walk through the Valley of Weeping it will become a place of springs where pools of blessing and refreshment collect after rains!"

Psalm 84:6

Perhaps you are suffering a deep hurt or sorrow right now. Or someone close to you is walking through the Valley of Weeping. These hurts and sorrows can and will become springs sending forth blessing and refreshment—that's God's promise! Believe it! Live it!

I am sure that someone close to you needs your encouragement today. Take the theme verse for today and rewrite it in your own words or in a way that would personalize it for a friend. Then take the time to share it with someone.

_____

_____

_____

_____

_____

_____

Through the tears I really believe God is creating pools of blessings and refreshment.

God Cares!

"Come to me, all who labor and are heavy laden, and I will give you rest."

Matthew 11:28 RSV

I recognized them in the crowd. They were long time friends of our family from the midwest. As they walked towards me, I recalled what had happened to their two sons that sad summer morning years ago. Their two boys were having fun on the lake when their makeshift raft fell apart and the youngest boy drowned. Then, only two years later, their other son was killed as he was pinned under a tractor that tipped over in the field.

I greeted them and then asked, "How did you find strength to carry on?" The mother answered bravely, "Someone in a far off state sent me a letter with a simple affirmation. It said, 'God still loves you!' I repeated that over and over and I still believe it!" Her eyes sparkled as she talked. Her husband stood there smiling through glossy eyes.

The three of us held hands and prayed. I watched them as they walked off—tall and trusting souls. God's iron pillared people!

Saint Paul understood. He wrote, "What can ever keep Christ's love from us? When we have trouble or calamity, when we are hunted down or destroyed, is it because he doesn't love us anymore? . . . NO . . . despite all this, overwhelming victory is ours through Christ who loved us enough to die for us." (Romans 8:35-37).

Nothing surprises me, for I am confident and strong through Christ!

God Cares!

"When you pass through the waters I will be with you; and through the rivers, they shall not overwhelm you; when you walk through fire you shall not be burned, and the flame shall not consume you. For I am the Lord your God!"

Isaiah 43:2, 3 RSV

During the first World War, a soldier in the trenches saw his friend out in no-man's land—that ground between his trench and the trench of the enemy. His friend lay there wounded.

The man asked his officer, "May I go, sir and bring him in?" The officer refused saying, "No one can live out there, and if you go I will only lose you as well."

Disobeying the officer, the man went to save his friend, for they had been like brothers throughout the war. Somehow, he managed to get his friend on his shoulder, stagger back to his trench, only to fall mortally wounded with his friend.

The officer was angry, "I told you not to go. Now I have lost two good men. It was not worth it!" With his dying breath the man said, "But it was worth it, sir, because when I got to him he said, 'Jim, I knew you'd come.' "

The distinct message of the cross of Jesus Christ is this: God will come to you when you cry out to Him, even to the point of giving His life to prove His faithfulness to you.

> **Lord Jesus, I look at your cross and I feel your love and care for me.**

God Saves!

"Serve each other with humble spirits, for God gives
special blessings to those who are humble."

1 Peter 5:5

St. Augustine spoke from the depths of a deep spiritual experience. As a wild, wanton, rebellious youth he deserted God, religion and faith. It was only when the emptiness of his life threatened to swallow him that he falteringly turned to God. He briefly prayed, "O God, forgive me of all my sins—but not yet."

And back he went to spend his youthful energies in immorality. Again, the hollowness of his unholy life over-whelmed him. With a sinking feeling he prayed again, "O God, forgive me for all my sins—save one." And again he left the place of prayer only to run again with the hares and dash with the hounds.

But total peace will only come from total commitment. And so he came back to the God who made him. Deeply, sincerely, humbly, resolutely he surrendered his life to Christ praying, "O God, forgive me for *all* my sins—and do it now. AMEN!"

Try praying this prayer. Mean it, and forgiveness, freedom and fellowship will dissolve your tensions like the warm summer sun evaporates the morning dew in the meadow.

I now have a beautiful feeling of peace
with God for I am forgiven!

God Saves!

"Humble yourselves before the Lord and he will exalt you."

James 4:10 RSV

How do you define sin? I was asked that question by a reporter recently. My answer was very simple: Traditionally sin has been defined as rebellion against God, an inner warfare, warfare between the self and God. But that is only the skin of sin. Think of sin as a golf ball. There is the outer skin, then there is the tight inner workings, and finally at the core of every ball is one solid, little, hard rubber pellet. The skin of sin is rebellion. The core is much deeper. What is the core of sin? It is our innate, inherited, negative self-image!

The negative self-image is responsible for any and all sin. God's toughest job is making you believe you are a beautiful, wonderful person through redemption and salvation! Believe God when he tells you how great you are!

What do you have trouble believing? Where in your life do you lack self-confidence and the feeling that you are an attractive person made by God? Write it down:

_____

_____

Now cover up what you have written with the words "God Loves Me!"

**Because God loves me,
I believe in myself!**

God Saves!

"Now change your mind and attitude to God and turn to him so he can cleanse away your sins and send you wonderful times of refreshment from the presence of the Lord."

Acts 3:19

I recently spent an evening with one of America's foremost psychiatrists, Dr. Karl Menninger. We were playing chess together in the Chicago home of a mutual friend, W. Clement Stone.

I was about to make my second move when the giant-minded Menninger glared at me over the chessboard and asked, "Dr. Schuller, do you preach repentance?"

I was taken aback, wondering what that question could possibly have to do with chess. Before I could answer, Dr. Menninger went on, saying, "Nothing will bring healing quicker to people than repentance. They are sinners. People know it. They are responsible for their own guilt! And they will never be healthy until they confess and repent before God!"

I was reminded of St. Paul's words to the men of Athens: " . . . Now he (God) commands all people everywhere to repent." (Acts 17:30 RSV).

Deep within, I feel the refreshing peace of God that is mine through Christ Jesus.

God Saves!

"So there is now no condemnation awaiting those who belong to Christ Jesus."

Romans 8:1

Have you ever been in a church where the minister scolds the people? He rebukes them, slaps his hands and pounds his fists, verbally crucifying those listening to him. I have attended churches like that. And the amazing thing is that the people go out and tell the preacher, "Oh, that was a great sermon, Reverend."

These people enjoyed being verbally spanked. They do not understand what the grace of God means. They do not really believe that when Christ died on the cross, he paid the price. All we have to do is accept!

But then, all of us have areas of our lives where we are still trying to earn God's forgiveness. There are some things in your life that you are still trying to hide from God. My message of grace to you is that God knows and he still loves you!

Now write your prayer as you thank God for setting you free through his grace.

Dear Lord, _____

_____

_____

Let me, O Lord, like a little child, dare to confess and then run with open arms to Your call of grace. Amen.

God Saves!

*"If anyone hears me calling him and opens the door, I will
come in and fellowship with him and he with me."*
                                        Revelations 3:20

I spoke with a young woman recently who showed me a
beautiful diamond ring that a certain young man had just
given her. She was excited! We taked about the future and
about the young man. Then I suggested that she make a
commitment of her life to Jesus Christ.

"What does that mean?" she asked me. I told her,
"Receiving Christ is pretty much like receiving that
diamond. You know what it means when you accept that
diamond engagement ring. It means you make a commitment to him and he makes a commitment to you. There is a
growing relationship between the two of you and you both
begin to build your whole future on that commitment. You
trust him and he trusts you. Now you share secrets with
him that you wouldn't share with anyone else, including
me."

She nodded her head and replied, "I understand and I
would like to make that kind of commitment to Jesus
Christ."

God offers you a diamond to wear on your heart and the
diamond's name is Jesus Christ. Accepting God's diamond
is as simple as opening a door when you've heard someone
knock. Invite Jesus Christ into your life and enjoy a future
rich in fellowship with God himself.

> God, I am committing my life to you
> and feel Your trust in me.

God Saves!

"Ask me and I will tell you some remarkable secrets."
                                        Jeremiah 33:3

The fourteenth chapter of John is an exciting chapter. Jesus Christ tells his disciples some amazing new possibilities available to them. He makes promises and asks several things of his followers. Read through the chapter again and make a list of what you do and a list of what Jesus promises.
I am to:
"Belive in Jesus" (vs. 12).

_____

_____

Jesus will:
"Make it possible for me to do greater things than he did." (vs. 12).

_____

_____

_____

_____

_____

> **Lord, I believe and I feel your power within helping me.**

God Saves!

"Create in me a new, clean heart, O God, filled with clean thoughts and right desires."

Psalm 51:10

I remember as a child rubbing a furry, soft peach against my cheek. It felt so soft and good. But when I turned the peach over, the backside was all raw and rough. It had been scraped by the scratchy splintered inside of a wooden bushel basket. As I looked at it I realized there was absolutely nothing I could do to restore its soft lustre.

You can take a violet blossom that feels just like velvet. You can pluck it, throw it down and trample it under your foot. But when you pick up the crushed velvety violet, nothing can restore it to its original beauty.

You cannot redeem or replace the scraped and bruised side of a fuzzy peach or crushed violet blossom. But God can restore your soul like new again! It is possible! It is happening all the time!

That's what the whole story of Christianity is about. God sent his son Jesus Christ into this world. As he said in Luke 19:10, "The Son of Man has come to seek and to save that which was lost" (NASB).

I sense God's power restoring and strengthening me. He is smoothing the rough places in my life. I am being redeemed.

God Will!

When it looks like I have failed
    I find myself asking "Lord, are you trying to
      tell me something?"
Failure doesn't mean I'm a failure.
    It does mean *I haven't succeeded yet!*
Failure doesn't mean I have accomplished nothing.
    It does mean *I have learned something!*
Failure doesn't mean I have been a fool.
    It does mean *I had enough faith to try!*
Failure doesn't mean I have been disgraced.
    It does mean *I dared to adventure!*
Failure doesn't mean I don't have it.
    It does mean *I have to do something in a
      different way.*
Failure doesn't mean I'm inferior.
    It does mean *I am not perfect!*
Failure doesn't mean I've wasted my life.
    It does mean *I have an excuse to start over
      again!*
Failure doesn't mean I should give up.
    It does mean *I must try harder!*
Failure doesn't mean I'll never make it.
    It does mean *I need more patience!*
Failure doesn't mean you have abandoned me, God.
    It does mean YOU MUST HAVE A BETTER IDEA!

"In everything you do, put God first,
and He will direct you and crown your
efforts with success."   Proverbs 3:6

God Will!

"Commit everything you do to the Lord. Trust him to help you do it and he will."

Psalm 37:5

The fear of failure keeps most people from believing that *God can and will make their dreams come true*. They are afraid to *try it*. I often think of Christy Wilson, that great missionary to Kabul, Afghanistan. The major industry in Kabul is raising sheep, and the major problem in raising sheep there is a disease caused by a worm that gets into the intestines of the sheep when they eat snails.

Now ducks love to eat these snails, but Christy noticed there were no ducks in Afghanistan. He wrote to a friend in the states and asked for some duck eggs. Twenty-four fertilized duck eggs were sent. His friend said, "They will hatch provided the eggs are not dropped, they get there on time and the temperature stays warm. In other words, it will take a miracle."

By the time they arrived in Kabul, some were broken, they were cracked and smelly. Christy had a dream. He said, "We'll just have to pray that we'll get at least one male and one female."

You can guess what happened: Only two eggs hatched, a male and a female. They multiplied and eventually wiped out the snails and the sheep industry boomed. God took Christy's dream and worked a miracle because he decided to *try it*.

> I have a dream. I am testing it to see if my positive dream is God's dream!

God Will!

"For your steadfast love is before my eyes, and I walk in faithfulness to thee."

Psalm 26:3 RSV

The second important principle that will help you grab hold of God's dream is to *Eye it*. Once your dream has passed the first test—you know it is a dream that God has placed in your mind—you now must visualize your dream. Write it down, outline it, or draw a picture. When you can see it in your mind, it becomes a fact!

Try it! Now Eye it! Write it down or draw a picture of your dream in the space below.

> **Today, my dream is becoming a possibility because I can visualize it!**

God Will!

"I am holding you by your right hand—I, the Lord your God—and I say to you, Don't be afraid; I am here to help you."

Isaiah 41:13

You've tried your dream and found that your positive idea is God's dream for your life. You've eyed it—either by writing it down or drawing a picture. Now it's time to *Buy it!* You make the commitment to be totally sold on the idea. You are willing to pay the price. Every great idea has a price attached to it.

I have found that when God has given me a great dream, there are always some negative thinkers around who will criticize the dream. Every time we have moved ahead to something great for God, I have been so convinced that it was God's idea that I would have gladly died for the success of the dream. Nothing can stop you when you know that it is God's dream for you!

Have you bought it! Are you committed to your dream as a good steward of God's great riches? Write out your commitment to the positive, life-changing dream you described yesterday: _____

_____

_____

_____

I am ready Lord, and I am eager to move ahead with our dream!

God Will!

*"They that wait upon the Lord shall renew their strength.
They shall mount up with wings like eagles; they shall run
and not be weary; they shall walk and not faint."*

Isaiah 40:31

Try it! Eye it! Buy it! Now it's time to *Fly it!* This simply
means the time has come for you to put strong wings on
your dream and start moving! Like a little boy with a kite,
start running and see if your dream can catch the wind.
Before you know it, your dream will be flying. People will
come to your support that you never dreamed would help.
It's true. Positive ideas and dreams attract support from
the most unexpected sources! But you must begin.

How? Simply make a list of the first three things you will
need to do to start to make your dream a reality. Then
start doing it.

To make my dream a reality, I will begin by:

1. _____

_____

2. _____

_____

3. _____

_____

I can sense it—my dream is happening.
God is giving me strength, wisdom and
power right now as I put wings to my dream.

God Will!

"I want you to trust me in your times of trouble, so I can rescue you, and you can give me glory."

Psalm 50:15

The fifth principle that will give you the confidence that God will help you make your dream come true is to *Tie it* down. DON'T QUIT!

One of the elders of our church suffered a severe heart attack about a year ago. It was a twenty-minute cardiac arrest. They got him to the hospital and he was in a comatose condition. One of the neurosurgeons said, "There's no hope for him. Even if he lives, he'll be a vegetable."

I came to his bedside shortly after his attack and remembered that Dr. Smiley Blanton, the eminent New York psychiatrist, had once said, "There are vast undamaged areas in the most severely damaged brain." I believed him. So I assumed that my church elder could hear and I said, "Stanley, this is Dr. Schuller. You're going to get well."

And a tear rolled down out of his eye! It was the first sign of hope! And Stanley got his dream, even in his comatose condition—the dream that he could recover.

Recently, Stan's wife drove him to the church and he walked around without crutches! I ran to him and hugged him. He said, "Pastor, you're great." I answered, "Stanley, God is great!"

Don't quit! Only you can kill God's dream for you. He will not let your dream come smashing down.

Lord, I feel like shouting because I am confident that together, we will succeed!

God Will!

"Those who trust in the Lord are steady as Mount Zion, unmoved by any circumstance."

Psalm 125:1

I enjoy the inspiring story of the Chinese farmer who had one son and one horse. One day the horse ran off to the hills. Everybody came and said, "Oh, you lost your horse; what bad luck! The old Chinese farmer replied, "How do you know it is bad luck?" And sure enough, that night the one horse came back and led twelve wild stallions with him. The one son closed the gate and the farmer had thirteen horses.

The neighbors came again and exclaimed, "Oh, what good luck!" The old farmer answered, "How do you know it is good luck?" And sure enough, as the one son was trying to break one of the wild stallions, he was thrown off and broke his leg. The neighbors lamented, "Oh, what bad luck." Again, the Chinese farmer questioned, "How do you know it is bad luck?"

A short time later a Chinese warlord came through town and drafted all the able-bodied young men and took them off to war with him. Those young men never returned. The old farmer's one son lived a long, full life.

Regardless of the circumstances, trust God. Your dream is his dream and his purpose is to turn you and me into servants, who are good stewards of his rich resources.

> Lord, forgive me for looking at circumstances. My eyes are on You and I am not distracted from my positive, life-changing dream.

Talking With God

"Speak Lord, for your servant hears."

1 Samuel 3:9 RSV

There are four kinds of prayer. One type of prayer is called petition. When you draft a request and go to God and say, "God, I want this," that's petition. For many people, this is the only kind of prayer they know.

How much of your praying would you estimate is spent in petition? _____

There is a second level of prayer called intercessory prayer, which means to intercede in the behalf of someone else. You pray for me and my needs, and I pray for you and your needs. We are both praying to God to help somebody else. This is intercession.

How much of your praying would you estimate is spent in intercessory prayer? _____

There is a third kind of prayer called praise and worship. When people who know God, love God and are so thankful that they pour out their hearts an in reverent words say, "Thank you, God," this is praise and worship.

How much of your praying would you estimate is spent in praise and worship? _____

But there is a fourth kind of prayer, Frank Laubach says, "Two-way prayer is the highest form of prayer." And that's the kind of prayer I want to consider with you the next few days.

Thank you, Lord, for the exciting ideas You are sending into my mind right now.

Talking With God

"Call to me and I will answer you, and will tell you great and hidden things which you have not known."
Jeremiah 33:3 RSV

Imagine that you are in a little boat near a sandy beach. You throw out an anchor and pull on the rope until you feel the sandy shore slide underneath. Then you step out onto the shore. What have you done? Have you moved the shore to the boat? No, you've moved the boat to the shore.

That's what real prayer is—not moving God to you in order to get something, but moving yourself closer to God in order to become something. You are close enough to listen to what He says to you.

Too many people think of prayer as a panic-stricken dashing to God, the all-powerful doctor, to get an immediate solution to their problem. Two-way prayer is much more. It involves listening to God as much as it is talking to God. God told the prophet Jeremiah, "Call to me and I will answer you." That's two-way prayer.

Who's been doing the talking in your prayer times? Describe what prayer is like in your life? _____

_____

_____

Lord, it's me. Today I am listening. Already I can begin to hear You as You answer the questions I have within.

Talking With God

"Be still, and know that I am God."

Psalm 46:10 RSV

I had never seen an avocado. I even went to college and took three years of postgraduate work, but I had never even heard of an avocado!

Then I moved to California and all kinds of people gave our family what I thought was one of the biggest, luscious, most unusual pears I'd ever seen. I tried every way to eat them, but finally gave up and ended up throwing them away. Fortunately, someone finally discovered my ignorance and showed me how to enjoy eating an avocado.

So many people have thrown prayer away the same way I threw all those avocados away. They talk to God and it doesn't work. So they give up. Let me describe how you can enjoy the experience of two-way prayer:

Begin by relaxing, closing your eyes and blocking out the distractions of the eye and the world. Meditate and focus your mind on something or some scene that will calm you. Then, when you are relaxed, quietly wait until you feel the stillness of God's presence with you.

Now ask the Holy Spirit to control your thinking so that God's thoughts and ideas will come into your mind. Then begin, in a humble, flexible attitude to ask God questions. As you ask each question, pause and wait for God to answer your question.

Lord, it's hard to shut off the noise around me, but I sense Your stillness and I am hearing Your voice. Thank you!

Talking With God

"Be still before the Lord, and wait patiently for him."
Psalm 37:7 RSV

They had three beautiful children. When the fourth was born, they were all excited. And then they found out the child was a mongoloid child. The mother said to me, "Dr. Schuller, we looked at this situation and saw it as an enormous, terrible problem. Our first reaction was one of anger, then bitterness, then self-pity. It was terrible.

"Then we heard you talk about two-way prayer on the Hour of Power. We went into two-way prayer and asked, 'Lord, could there be any good in what has happened to us?' And we waited. We heard a thought in our minds and the thought was very strong. 'Yes.' Then we asked, 'God, what good could possibly come out of this problem?' And this sentence came to my mind, 'I will teach you a new dimension of love!' Wow! That changed everything! What has happened in our lives since then has been a miracle.

Two-way prayer is going into a quiet place to talk to God and asking Him questions. You don't spill out your problems necessarily. You don't make a lot of statements. You don't ask for demands. You don't go forward with pitiful appeals. You go with questions and wait patiently for God to answer. This is mountain-moving prayer!

My spirit is refreshed and renewed as I am quiet before the Lord.

Talking With God

*"I will bless the Lord who counsels me; he gives me
wisdom in the night. He tells me what to do."*

Psalm 16:7

There is mountain-moving power in two-way prayer. In
order to see the mountain-moving power at work, you
must see the mountains. A mountain-moving prayer
notebook will help you see the power available through
two-way prayer. Start below and then continue to add to
your list in a separate notebook.

My Question	God's Answer	Steps taken by me

Today, I am taking the steps God is
telling me to take in order to move
mountains.

Talking With God

"Let the words of my mouth and the meditation of my heart be acceptable in your sight, O Lord, my rock and my redeemer."

Psalm 19:14 RSV

I spent several hours one time with Dr. Viktor Frankl discussing the bundle of emotions and variety of forces within us that we do not understand. I discussed with this eminent psychiatrist the force of meditation. We do not understand this great force, but meditation, when effective, is the proper harnessing by humans of divine laws created within the human structure for holy and high purpose.

Now, this great force of meditation can be destructive when used improperly. But Christian meditation has been practiced for centuries, all the way back to the psalmists and the patriarchs. You don't need to pay a fee or find a guru. Possibility thinking meditation—two-way prayer meditation—focuses on Jesus Christ. Use the words, "I AM" with each breath as you relax if you want help in closing out the distracting sounds while in meditative prayer.

Two-way prayer meditation really works. It creates a mind-set where God can send His signal through to you. You can achieve a sense of oneness with God. He is close enough to you so that He literally speaks to you!

I feel a quietness within my spirit—
no distractions, only God and me,
talking together.

Talking With God

"I will keep on expecting you to help me. I praise you more and more."

Psalm 71:14

Some of you are going to make major decisions today. It may effect your family, your job, or your destiny. Try two-way prayer! "But," you protest, "How do I know that what I hear is God speaking to me?" Let me suggest four steps you can take to answer that question.

First, repeat your question in two or three different two-way prayer conversations. If the answer you have received is from God, it will be the same each time.

Second, Possibilitize. Believe that it is possible for God to speak to you because you have asked Him to speak to you. Believe that!

Third, Compare your answer with what God has already told you in His Holy Bible. God's message to you in two-way prayer will not be different than His message to you in scripture.

Fouth, Actualize. The purpose of two-way prayer is to get God's message into your mind so that you can go out and act. Do what God wants you to do to make your life and your world a more beautiful place.

Let's try it now, again. Close your eyes, and begin to meditate. Relax and be very informal and open with God. Ask Him questions about your major decisions. When you finish, write down God's answer.

> Thank you Lord, for Your messages that come from the deepest, unexplored, unfathomable seas of silence. I am listening. I will act.

Self-Love

"You Lord, . . . have placed a crown of glory and honor upon my head."

Psalm 8:5

Once, when I challenged an impossibility thinker to become a possibility thinker, his answer provided me with a new revelation. "It's not worth the effort," he said. As he spoke to me, I studied his eyes and I knew he didn't mean what he said. He really meant to say, "I'm not worth it." I immediately dropped the idea of converting him into a possibility thinker.

Instead, I went to work attempting to build up in his mind a picture of his enormous worth as a person. Then little by little, when he began to stop hating himself and started liking himself, he came alive. He became a possibility thinker!

I can boldly say to you, no matter what has happened in your life you are not a complete failure, a hopeless sinner or a total washout. I can't begin to count how many times I have heard people in my study tell me those exaggerated distorted and destructive lies. Everytime I was able to see and point out worthwhile qualities in the person who was condemning himself unfairly, unreasonably and unlovingly.

God loves you and so do I. And it is good and right for you to say, "God loves me and so do I!" Everytime a negative or critical thought about yourself enters your mind today, repeat that sentence to yourself.

God loves me and He knows all my secrets. Because God loves me I can love me!

Self-Love

"We know that God has chosen you."

1 Thessalonians 1:4

Saint Paul warned his readers at Rome that they were to "Be honest in your estimate of yourselves." (Romans 12:3). It is not part of Christianity to put yourself down! But it's a lot easier than being honest about your good qualities. Today is a good time to begin making an honest list of your good characteristics. Start by listing at least six good and positive qualities about yourself. If you find it difficult, ask someone close to you to help you and write down everything they say.

A POSITIVE ESTIMATE OF MYSELF

1. _____

2. _____

3. _____

4. _____

5. _____

6. _____

I am a person of value for God has created me and loves me.

Self-Love

*"You are the world's seasoning, to make it tolerable . . .
You are the world's light . . . glowing in the night for all to
see."*

Matthew 5:13, 14

It was a majestic sight to see the good earth bearing a
heavy harvest of grain and corn. Not an acre was wasted.
Every piece of land put to good use.

Then we came to the bleak and barren foothills of the
great Rocky Mountains. These rugged peaks greet the
traveler like granite sentinels standing guard at the
gateway to the West. We began to climb the twisting road
that winds like a snake up the mountainside. Finally we
reached a point where we could look to the west and see
the beautiful but unproductive mountains and to the east
where unfolding below on the endless plains was the rich
farmland with little lakes and rivers shimmering. What a
contrast!

When we stopped for gas, I made the mistake of point-
ing at the mountains and commenting to the station atten-
dant, "What a lot of worthless land." The young man
looked up at me and firmly stated, "That is *not* wasteland.
There are minerals in those rocks and there may be oil. We
believe there is uranium in those mountains also. We just
haven't found it yet!

Jesus looks at you and sees the tremendous potential that
can be unlocked if you will only believe in yourself.

I am somebody! I feel the greatness
within me stirring as I believe in myself
as Jesus Christ believes in me.

Self-Love

*"So God made man like his Maker. Like God did God
make man; Man and maid did he make them."*
Genesis 1:27

I heard of a teacher in a public school in one of the inner
city areas who said to her students, "Today, we are going
to study identity." She went up to a little black boy and
said, "Johnny, we're studying identity. Who are you?" He
stood up and said, "Well, I know my name is Johnny and I
know I'm black. I also know I'm good—'cause God don't
make no junk!"

Johnny was one of God's super-living-people. He was
confident because He knew he was God's creation. When
you know you are God's child, you know who you are!

Johnny had a good answer to an important question—
"Who are you?" The psalmist David had an answer in
Psalm 139. If that teacher walked up to you today and
asked the same question, how would you answer?

Write down your answer: _____

_____

_____

_____

I am God's friend. God loves me.
If God has chosen me for His friend, I
must be a marvelous person. I am!

Self-Love

"Who dares accuse us whom God has chosen for his own?"
Romans 8:33

Jesus Christ always tried to give man's self-image a boost. When he met immoral people He never called them sinners. Never! One of the most despised members of His society was the Jew named Zacchaeus, who was a tax-collecting tool of the Romans. When Jesus met him, He could have judged him harshly. Instead, He sought to build this man's sense of self-love by offering to spend the night at his house. As a result, Zacchaeus started to love himself again.

Dr. Sam Shoemaker once said, "Christ alone fills the human heart with love—joy—peace—self-confidence. No wonder a genuine Christian really loves himself."

Take a look at the people in your life. Look at them through the positive, loving, affirming eyes of Jesus Christ. What do you see? Whose self-image could you help build up? Write down their name:_____.
Now describe the first thing you are going to do with that person. Be specific._____

_____

_____

Today, I give love and encourage
self-love in the people I meet.

Self-Love

A Rebirth of Self-worth awaits you. When that happens you will be:

> Poised instead of tense
> Confident instead of confused
> Bold instead of timid
> Enthusiastic instead of bored
> Successful instead of failing
> Energetic instead of fatigued
> Agreeable instead of cantankerous
> Positive instead of negative
> Self-forgiving instead of self-condemning
> Self-respecting instead of self-disgusting.

Self-Love

"As we live in Christ, our love grows more perfect and complete."

1 John 4:17

I attended the commencement of one of the Christian colleges nearby. In the small select group of outstanding students were three persons who immediately stood out from the others. One was a black man, one was an Indian, and one was a blind girl with a white cane.

All three of them graduated Magna Cum Laude! All three were listed in Who's Who in American Colleges and Universities, along with other honors and distinctions. And, I am sure that all three could have been miserable failures, blaming their disadvantaged childhood, or a prejudiced society. But the fact was, three people, each with strikes against them, made it to the top!

Some people make victims of their disadvantages— others become victimized by their disadvantages. What is the difference? The black man, the Indian, the blind girl— all had one thing in common. They believed in themselves because they believed in the power of Jesus Christ. They believed that Jesus Christ could change their life and their situation.

When you believe in Jesus Christ—believe that he loves you and died for you—you also begin to believe that with Him you can reach the top! You deserve to reach the top!

> **Because I have self-love, I have self-worth. I have the confidence to turn my problems into personal triumphs.**

Peak to Peek

"Tomorrow . . . I will stand at the top of the hill, with the rod of God in my hand."

Exodus 17:9

Many of you have read the story of Tara, the daughter of the producer of the Hour of Power. Tara suffered a brain injury which left her deaf, dumb and blind. It looked like she would be a vegetable all her life. But today, six years later, she can see, she can hear, she can speak perfectly, but still she cannot walk.

Several months ago, her dad called with exciting news. For the first time Tara got on her hands and knees and began to creep. He excitedly said, "She held herself up for about 30 seconds on her own hands and knees." Tara experienced a new perspective—previews of great things to come. She raised her head and saw things in a way she had not seen them before. She had a *peak* to *peek* experience!

Tara's peak experience was like a mountain-top-experience. Her *peak* was holding herself up on her hands and knees. As she did this, she had a *peek* experience—a peek or a glimpse of possible future experiences. Tara has a new vision of what she can be and what she can do.

A *peak* experience is a positive, self-affirming experience. It is a self-expanding experience that tells me I CAN. And the I CAN always leads to a new consciousness, or peek of what I can be and do.

Today, with God's help I will climb my mountain and see what great things God has planned for me.

Peak to Peek

"Where there is no vision, the people perish."
                                    Proverbs 29:18 KJV

Have you ever noticed how some people's lives seem to be one success unfolding upon another? Every new achievement seems to be one up on the last success. That's the way their life incredibly unfolds. The achievement level continues to escalate and climb. How do you explain it? Knowingly or unknowingly these persons have tapped into a vital principle that I call the "peak to peek" principle.

Now a peak experience gives you a new vision of greater accomplishments that you can experience and attempt. A peak experience affirms to you who you are and leaves you with an awareness that you are more than you ever thought you were.

For a child—and for Tara—creeping is a peak experience. Later when the child stands with two feet and takes the first few faltering steps and succeeds, this also becomes a peak experience.

When you stand at the top of the mountain you can see a new dream in your new vision. The dream gives rise to desire, the desire gives rise to the daring-to-do, the daring-to-do gives rise to the deciding-to-begin! And that's the road to success.

The Bible says that God blesses faith. Have faith in your dream.

I am daring to dream God's dream for me today. I feel the exhilaration of climbing God's mountain!

Peak to Peek

"For whatever does not proceed from faith is sin."
                                    Romans 14:23 RSV

What have been the peak experiences in your life? Think back over the past few years and make a note of those experiences which have inspired you and given you a vision of what God has in store for your tomorrow. Write down at least three vision-expanding success-producing experiences:

1. _____

_____

_____

2. _____

_____

_____

3. _____

_____

_____

> Today, I am standing on the mountaintop. God is at my side and I am beginning to see new valleys to explore. By faith, I am succeeding!

Peak to Peek

"In the same way, we can see and understand only a little about God now, as if we were peering at his reflection in a poor mirror; but someday we are going to see him in his completeness, face to face."

1 Corinthians 13:12

The self-centered person has to grow in unselfishness before God will say "GO."

The cautious person must grow in courage before God will say "GO."

The reckless person must grow in carefulness before God will say "GO."

The timid person must grow in confidence before God will say "GO."

The self-belittling person must grow in self-love before God will say "GO."

The dominating person must grow in sensitivity before God will say "GO."

The critical person must grow in tolerance before God will say "GO."

The negative person must grow in positive attitude before God will say "GO."

The power-hungry person must grow in kindness and gentleness before God will say "GO."

The pleasure-seeking person must grow in compassion for suffering people before God will say "GO."

And the God-ignoring soul must become a God-adoring soul before God will say "GO."

I feel patient as I wait expectantly for God's guidance and direction.

Peak to Peek

*"But as for me, I will sing each morning about your power
and mercy. For you have been my high tower of refuge."*
                                                        Psalm 59:16

A psychologist and I were talking about a person we
were both interested in helping. This person's whole life
was one set of problems after another. He was what you
would call a born loser.

The psychologist hit it right on the head when he said,
"The trouble with this person is that he has never had a
peak experience." He's never had an experience in really
succeeding. So he's convinced that he is born a failure.

This young man failed in school, failed in teenage
relationships, failed in sociological relationships, failed in
his first job, got fired from his second job and landed in a
reform school. And that's been his basic lifestyle all along.
His last peak experience was when he learned to walk!

How can he have a peak experience? There is no way it
can happen without the kind of dynamic religious experience we call "establishing a relationship with God." That's
where he must begin.

Has it been a long time since you had a mountaintop
experience? Where do *you* begin? I suggest you begin by
making sure that your relationship with God is solid and
strong. You can only stand on the mountain peak with
God! He gives you a peek at your tomorrows!

From the peak I can see greater
possibilities!

Peak to Peek

"For God is at work within you . . . helping you to do what he wants."

Philippians 2:13

A couple of days ago I knew I had to get out and run. I wanted to run. I knew I should run. But I wasn't in the mood to run the six miles I usually run.

My home is six miles from the church, so I got into my running suit and decided, "I'm only going to run half way from the house to the church." When I got to that point, what could I do? I couldn't hitch-hike home. I had to finish, there was no other way.

I use this principle a lot in my life. When I know there is something I should do and can't see doing the whole thing, I only make the commitment to go as far as the point of no return. Then I'm caught— I have to complete the job.

Some of you may be afraid to begin climbing your mountain. You don't think you can finish. You're thinking—"Can I make it; can I succeed?" Decide to begin and then decide to keep going. Don't worry about the top, just decide to get started. The key is in deciding to begin.

What's keeping you from climbing to your mountain peak? What are you involved in now that could be a peak experience for you?

I am climbing to the peak. I can feel the clean air and I will keep going until I reach the top!

Peak to Peek

When the idea is not right;
   God says, "NO!"
When the time is not right;
   God says, "SLOW!"
When you are not right;
   God says, "GROW!"
When everything is right;
   God says, "GO!"

"I will instruct you, says the Lord, and guide you along the best pathway for your life; I will advise you and watch your progress."   **Psalms 32:8**

Discover Yourself

"For I can do everything God asks me to with the help of Christ who gives me the strength and power."

Philippians 4:13

How do you succeed? You succeed by hook and by crook! Now before you misunderstand, let me explain the meaning of that phrase — by hook and by crook.

I fish once in a while, but there has never been a time when the fish jumped into my boat. I'm a great believer in positive thinking, but the fish simply will not jump into the boat. I have to try. I must make the effort. I have to throw the fish hook into the water.

That's the *hook* in our phrase. The hook means I do everything I can and then trust God to do the rest. The hook is a balance between trying and trusting.

The crook refers to the shepherds staff with the curved handle. This is a very handy tool for the shepherd. If one of the lambs start to stray, he reaches out with his long staff and with the curved end gently nudges the lamb back to the flock.

Or if one of the sheep falls into a ravine, or other difficult place to escape, the shepherd hooks his crook underneath the lamb and lifts it to safety.

So the *crook* in our phrase means that as we try and make the effort to succeed, Jesus Christ, our shepherd, has his crook at hand to guard us and rescue us from danger. So we can succeed by hook and by crook!

> **By hook and by crook I am becoming what God wants me to be!**

Discover Yourself

"You are close beside me, guarding, guiding all the way."
Psalm 23:4

God has been helping you discover the person you can be by hook and by crook. Stop and reflect back on your life. Where has God helped you use the hook? Where has he used the shepherd's crook?

God used the *hook* in my life when He _____

_____

_____

_____

_____

_____

God used the *crook* in my life when He _____

_____

_____

_____

_____

> Today, a more beautiful me is coming through. More and more, I am becoming the person I want to be!

Discover Yourself

"For God is at work within you, helping you want to obey him, and then helping you do what he wants."

Philippians 2:13

I found myself traveling back to Russia some time ago. This time my wife joined me on the visit. We were touring Leningrad together when we met a very sharp young Communist woman. I was so impressed with her that I could easily picture her as the wife of some future premier of that country.

She asked, "What kind of work do you do?" "Well," I answered, "I am a minister." Then I prayed and asked God what I could say next. What he inspired me to say to her is equally applicable to you. I continued, "You know, I have studied both theology and psychology for some years now, and I can declare as a fact this principle: Any person — whether a Capitalist, a Communist, a Russian or an American — any person will change and will become more beautiful inside if he or she will become a believer in Jesus Christ. That's a fact!"

She was speechless as her face revealed for a moment that she was captured by this authoritative, unchallengeable law which can be scientifically proven.

You will become a more beautiful person when you become a beautiful believer in Jesus Christ. There is a more beautiful *you* waiting to come through!

> **Thank you, God, for doing something beautiful in my mind, my heart, and in my life today!**

Discover Yourself

"It is God himself who has made us what we are and given us new lives from Christ Jesus."

Ephesians 2:10

I know what kind of person I would be if Jesus Christ did not live within me. How about you? What kind of person would you be if the Spirit of Christ had never entered your life? Let's take a positive inventory.

Without Christ, I would be	With Christ, I am becoming

God's power now flows through me, quickening, strengthening and developing within me joy and beauty!

Discover Yourself

"God's unchanging plan has always been to adopt us into his own family by sending Jesus Christ to die for us. And he did this because he wanted to!"

Ephesians 1:5

"I must tell you my story," the 63 year old woman said to me. "I was 13 when I became an atheist. I had experienced something terrible and I prayed and prayed to God about it. But instead of going away, my problem got worse than ever. So then and there I decided there was no God.

"My husband and I have been married for 42 years. All those years he was a believer and would faithfully attend church. But I would never listen to him. I don't know how he put up with me.

"But," she continued, "one Sunday morning after my husband left for church, I listened to you on the TV set. Something about the way you twinkled kept me from turning you off. You talked about Jesus and His love. I felt something inside that seemed very real. I still couldn't put my hand on God, but as I listened, I prayed and invited Jesus into my life. I changed right there! I could hardly wait to tell my husband when he came home."

By this time, both she and her husband were crying as they went on to describe the beautiful person she really was. Almost fifty years as an atheist, and only recently she has discovered faith and in the same process she discovered herself! When you are related to Jesus Christ, you can discover the beautiful person you really are!

I greet today related to Jesus Christ. He makes both me and my day beautiful!

Discover Yourself

"I can never be lost to your Spirit, I can never get away from my God!"

Psalm 139:7

"How do I get close to God?" Those words came from a corporate executive sitting next to me in a plane. "Have you ever asked Jesus Christ to come into your life?" I asked. He replied, "No, that sounds too simple. I'm sorry, I can't buy that."

"Well," I said, "it is simple, just like the sunlight every day, a child's hug and kiss or the blossom of a flower. When God does something He doesn't make it complicated. Why don't we pray right now about it?"

"Right here?" he questioned. "Why not?" And so we held hands and prayed, and this great big tough executive was crying with real tears rolling down his face as he said, "It's true, It's real!"

Have you ever discovered this? What is holding you back from trusting God for some problem or inviting Jesus Christ to come into your life? Try to describe it in words:

_____

_____

_____

_____

Now look at what you have written. You're trying to make things complicated, I am certain. Believe in the simplicity of God's solution! Believe!

> **I am simply thrilled today as God works in and through me!**

Discover Yourself

"But whenever anyone turns to the Lord from his sins, then the veil is taken away. The Lord is the Spirit who gives them life, and where he is there is freedom."

2 Corinthians 3:16, 17

"Hi! How are you?" I asked the young girl behind the candy counter. "I don't really know," she replied. "You don't look very enthused," I commented.

As she handed me my newspaper, she said, "I'm not very happy. I left Vietnam with my three small children after my husband was killed in the fighting. I miss my country and the rest of my family, but I can't go back." And tears began to flow down her cheek.

"Do you have a faith or religion?" I asked. "I'm Buddhist," she replied, fighting back the tears. "But I don't practice my religion."

"Do you mind if I share with you what Jesus Christ means to me?" I asked again. When she asked what I meant, I continued, "Well, He died on a cross for you and me, but He rose again and lives today! He's alive! He's the only religious leader who ever said, 'I will die for you.' And today He lives within me and I feel love inside of me because of what Jesus does for me. Would you like to know Jesus Christ like that?"

Hesitating at first, she said, "I think so. Nobody has ever asked me before. Yes, I would." And so in the lobby of the hotel, we held hands and prayed. She invited Jesus Christ into her life. Her face was absolutely transformed!

Now I am free of all negative thoughts! Thank you, Lord, for the added blessing of freedom.

It's Possible

When faced
with a mountain
I WILL NOT QUIT
I will keep on striving until
I climb over, find a pass through
tunnel underneath—or simply
stay and turn the mountain
into a gold mine,
with God's help!

It's Possible

"If you have faith, and don't doubt, you can do things like this and much more."

Matthew 21:21

John Roebling was the engineer with the idea of bridging the river and tying Manhattan Island with Brooklyn. It was a fabulous idea, but all the bridge-building experts and structural engineers said it was impossible. Some agreed that the river might be spanned, but that a 1,595 foot span would never stand up against the winds and the tides. But John Roebling and his son, Washington figured out how the problems could be solved and how the obstacles would be overcome.

And then, as construction began, John Roebling was killed on the job and in the same accident, Washington suffered the bends underneath the water. The son survived, but was left with permanent brain damage, so that he never walked or talked again.

Everybody said to forget the project. But not Washington. He developed a code of communication by touching one finger to the arm of his wife. And he communicated the dream through her to the engineers on the project. For thirteen years, Washington Roebling supervised construction that way. And finally in 1883 traffic streamed across the completed Brooklyn Bridge. When Washington Roebling was told the news, he wept for joy. The impossible dream became a reality!

> God, You are helping me right now
> discover the great possibilities
> You have planted within me.

It's Possible

"Accept our praise, O Lord, for all your glorious power.
We will write songs to celebrate your mighty acts!"
                                          Psalm 21:13

Everyone is faced, from time to time, with problems that appear to be impossible to solve. A key to successful living is to plan everyday with two questions: 1) What is the biggest problem I'm facing today? 2) What will I do about it today? Keep that up everyday and you'll be surprised where you're at a year from now! Briefly describe your "impossible problem."

_____

_____

_____

Now I want you to practice possibility thinking. For some of you, it may seem futile and very difficult. But I want you to make the effort! Look again at the problem you just described. Now complete the following statement.
IT MIGHT BE POSSIBLE IF _____

_____

_____

The "if" is fading away and I can
feel my faith growing. I believe
it is possible!

It's Possible

"I am sure that he who began a good work in you will bring it to completion at the day of Jesus Christ."
                                        Philippians 1:6 RSV

One night the Berkshire Boys found themselves at the edge of the a stream where they were caught off guard by the Confederates. Fleeing across the bridge to the other side, the commander discovered that he had left his sword in his tent. Before he could start back, a teenager named Johnny Ring, said to him, "Colonel, let me go for it, sir."

Johnny Ring ran across the bridge, got the sword out of the tent and started back. When he reached the bridge, flames were licking at the edges of the boards, but he ran across without hesitating, and he dropped the sword at his commander's feet. He was badly burned and lay there dying. Colonel Conwell, an atheist, looked at him and wept, saying, "Johnny, I'm sorry, I'm sorry!"

Johnny replied, "Don't be sorry, sir. I'm not afraid to die. I know Jesus Christ and I'll be all right." With his dying breath he asked, "Colonel, are you afraid to die?" "Yes," replied the commander.

Beside Johnny's body that night, the commander knelt down, and in a great moment alone, he invited Jesus Christ into his life as his Saviour. As he knelt, he made a vow that he would become the minister that Johnny wanted to be. He told God that he would work sixteen hours a day—eight for Johnny and eight for himself. Conwell became one of the great ministers of his day.

I am an instrument of God's peace
and God's possibilities.

It's Possible

"If God is on our side, who can ever be against us?"
                                          Romans 8:31

Colonel Conwell, after becoming a minister, began to lecture across the country. His lecture was entitled, "Acres of Diamonds." He said, "There are acres of diamonds in the problem that you have before you right now."

He delivered that lecture over 6,000 times and earned more than six million dollars. With that money he built Temple University, in Philadelphia. He believed "It was possible!"

What great thing is God attempting to do through you? An interesting experience is yours if you will complete the following sentence:

If I knew I couldn't fail, I would _____

_____

_____

_____

_____

_____

_____

I have a strong feeling that
everything is going to work out because
I am on the Lord's side!

It's Possible

"The Lord is my strength, my song, and my salvation."
                                                    Exodus 15:2

I'll never know to what extent being born an Iowa farm boy made me the possibility thinker I am today. I don't think anything is more exciting than springtime on a farm.

I remember many years when Dad needed all the grain of last year's crop to feed the cattle and the livestock. But there was one little corner of our cornbin where there was grain, and Dad would never touch it. I would say to him, "But, Dad, you still have some grain in there." And he would say, "No, that is next year's seed corn, and I cannot use it for feed." So he saved it. Then the spring came. How desperately he needed every kernel to feed the livestock. But what did he do? He buried it in the ground.

Now suppose my father had studied the odds. Let's suppose he had said, "Let's see, I've got a kernel of corn. If I feed it to the cattle, I know it will be productive. I can be sure of it. There is no risk. On the other hand, I can plant it in the ground, but that's filled with risk. Weeds could choke it, birds could eat it, it could rot, or the hail and winds could destroy it just as it starts to grow. It could be worthless. It's risky to put it in the ground. But it just might multiply a hundredfold!"

Don't wait because something is risky. Break loose and *begin before it's possible*. Only then will your dream really become a possibility!

I am making my decisions on
God's ability, not on my ability.

It's Possible

"I am convinced that . . . nothing will ever be able to separate us from the love of God demonstrated by our Lord Jesus Christ when he died for us."

Romans 8:38, 39

I have occasionally been criticized for my "slogans," but they have been an important part of making me whatever success I am today. I remember sitting in the bank at the age of twelve as my father did some business. I sat there and memorized the slogan on the bank calendar. Over the years I have changed it a bit to read:

GREAT PEOPLE ARE COMMON PEOPLE WHO DARE TO MAKE UNCOMMON COMMITMENTS TO GOD.

God's great people are great because of their commitment to a goal. They are committed to some beautiful God-inspired dream. I invite you to be one of God's great people. Make a commitment today. Write it down so you can look back at it for inspiration when the going gets rough. Take the risk!

My Commitment

_____

_____

_____

My problems are possibilities, my obstacles are opportunities because I am committed to God and to greatness!

The Future

"Your goodness and unfailing kindness shall be with me all of my life, and afterwards I will live with you forever in your home."

Psalm 23:6

The surgical ward was a crude shop. The heat was stifling. The odors almost overwhelmed the visiting American minister. But the steady missionary doctor kept at his task with untiring skill.

After seven hours the missionary doctor stood up, faced Dr. Evans, and announced that the job was done. They walked back to the modest office and Dr. Evans asked the missionary, "How much would you have been paid for that operation in America?" Probably five hundred dollars," the doctor answered.

Evans said, "I'm curious. How much do you get for that operation here?" The doctor picked up from his desk a dented copper coin and said, "Well, to begin with—this. The patient came into our mission holding this coin and with tears in her eyes asked me, 'Doctor, do you suppose this would pay for an operation?' I looked at her and said, 'I think so!' " The doctor went on as tears filled his eyes, "Most of all it makes me feel so good inside knowing that my hands for a few hours have been the hands of Jesus Christ healing a sick woman."

What about the future? If you want a full life, you have to pour it out. Involvement is the only indulgence that really satisfies!

> **My faith unlocks the door of limitation and replaces the fear of the future with the activity of love.**

The Future

"If I ride the morning winds to the farthest oceans, even there your hand will guide me."

Psalm 139:9

As I watched, I noticed that some daring swimmers were trying to see if they could "ride the waves," the huge mountainous waves which came crashing in on the beaches. As I watched, several of these would-be swimmers got into the water and stumbled through the foamy shallows, but were too slow. They were overtaken, upset, flattened and sent sputtering in the surf by the liquid mountain.

Farther out in the deep, I saw a skillful rider of the surf as he carefully watched the wave as it was building, swelling and rising. Instead of running from the wave, he rode the graceful curve of the growing mountain of water. Instead of being flattened, he was lifted! Instead of being made low, he rose high and was carried far!

Every trouble has vast built-in opportunities to grow, to learn, to serve, or to be cleansed. Imagination can turn your bed of trouble into fruitful pastures. Your time of lying low can become your morning of spiritual refreshment. Wait patiently for the Lord. He will not mock your waiting. God will not laugh at your praying. Suddenly, you will feel the mighty hand of God underneath you and all around you, as He lifts you and guides you into your future!

I feel a mysterious, calm, quiet, tranquil assurance for the future rising deep within my being. What a relief! Thank you, Lord!

The Future

"No eye has seen, nor ear heard, nor the heart of man conceived, what god has prepared for those who love him."

1 Corinthians 2 : 9 RSV

In Judges 7, Gideon wanted to be certain about his future, so he put out some wool on the threshing floor and asked God to make the wool wet and the floor dry. His fear was so real that when God answered Gideon, it wasn't enough. Gideon had to repeat the process again another night asking God to do just the opposite.

If Gideon feared the future, then you do not need to be ashamed if you have fears about your future. Gideon did something constructive about his fear. Write down what it is about the future that creates within you a feeling of fear.

_____

_____

_____

_____

Now read over what you have written, and then read the verse for today. Can God handle your future? Believe He can—God CAN!

> **The future is my friend because God is in my future just as He is with me now.**

The Future

"For the Lord watches over all the plans and paths of godly men."

Psalm 1:6

I like the attitude of my neighbor. She and her husband worked, saved, and in their fifties bought a lovely home near ours. Suddenly, one week after they moved, her husband, without warning, died of a heart attack! And she was left alone with a large new home.

I stopped and talked with her one morning. She was out in the yard surveying the boxes, barrels and unpotted plants. The morning sun was bright and she looked wide awake as she took stock of the work that needed to be done. You know what gives me great strength?" she said to me, "It is the certain assurance that it was my husband's time to go. It was God's will. And it is His will for me to get these plants in the ground and things unpacked!"

And she meant it! I watched her as she helped the neighborhood children collect old newspapers for the local school. She was laughing and having a grand time. Soon after that, she was in our home for coffee and said, "Oh, sometimes I cry—but it was God's will. And I know He loves me. He does nothing wrong."

Her life has not stopped. Her future is alive. As I watch her, I remember these words, "I had fainted, unless I had believed to see the goodness of the Lord in the land of the living." (Psalm 27:13 KJV).

**This one thing I know—
God is for me! I am not afraid!**

The Future

I have a strong, serene feeling
that
God is planning something good for me today,
I cannot explain it,
but
I have a deep feeling
that wonderful things are in store for me.

I am expecting God to surprise me
with his tender mercy.

Thank you, Lord
for
each of my tomorrows!

Amen!

The Future

"I will be your God through all your lifetime . . . I made you and I will care for you."

Isaiah 46:4

The hand of the Almighty is never far away. No wonder you can trust the future! And when you cannot see any good, but only stark, naked, cruel, brutal tragedy in a catastrophic situation, then you can expect God to come and show mercy!

As an unexpected gust of wind comes under the weary wings of a storm-drenched bird to lift the pitiful creature to higher altitudes where it can soar in new strength, so God comes with unannounced invasions of mercy!

Often, God will use people as his messengers of mercy. I am certain that you can recall times when God sent someone to you at the right moment with words of encouragement. Perhaps God wants to use you in that way today.

Stop and relax. Enter into two-way prayer with God. Ask Him if there is someone that He would like you to visit, or call, or send a note of encouragement. Write down their name: _____

What does God want you to do? _____

_____

_____

> **God, here I am. Use me as the bearer of mercy to someone who is hurting today.**

The Future

*"May God bless you richly and grant you increasing
freedom from all anxiety and fear."*

1 Peter 1:2

As I returned from New York, the giant jumbo jet circled
into the landing path at Los Angeles. As we completed our
cross-country flight, those last miles presented a kaleido-
scope of scenery; Catalina Island lying off the coast in the
dark blue Pacific; the white surf on the Southern California beaches; the snow-capped mountains surrounding the
Los Angeles basin; and beyond those majestic mountain
peaks; the vast expanse of desert.

I have made the flight often and have frequently noticed
a tiny square patch of green in the middle of that
seemingly endless desert wasteland—a thriving little farm
surrounded by a thirsty monster of shifting sand. Will the
defenseless little ranch be swallowed up by the parched
desert on some future flight? I doubt it. For this fertile oasis
draws its life from deep wells that tap a subterranean river.
Far to the west, the snow on the mountains melt and the
water streams silently down the eastern slope, draining
deep into the sand to feed the subterranean river. The
future of the ranch is quite safe, for it has a secret alliance
with the mountain!

So it is with you. Your life is in the care and keeping of
God who keeps watch over His own. You are an island
surrounded by an unfriendly sea, a patch of green in a
desert wasteland.

> **My roots run deep and tap into God's
> rich supply. I can feel God's confidence
> surging within. I have nothing to fear!**

God-Power Within

*"In everything you do, put God first, and he will direct you
and crown your efforts with success!"*

Proverbs 3:6

You can explode with achievement if you have God-power within you. This is absolutely true. It can be reduced to a simple lesson in what I call religious mathematics, or the mathematics of faith.

Faith is a mathematical power! It subtracts weakness; adds power, divides difficulties, multiplies possibilities! What a way to live!

You can see this principle at work in the life of Jesus Christ. He was the most successful person who ever lived. He never had a negative, defeating thought. I try to think positively, but there are times when I become negative.

Now someone will say that Jesus was a failure because He died on a cross. But nothing could be further from the truth. The key is in your definition of success. I define success as fulfilling God's plan for your life. Success is achieving what God wants you to achieve.

Jesus was the world's greatest success because He perfectly did what God wanted Him to do. Don't be afraid of success! God wants you to succeed!

> **Through the activity of God's power
> within me, I succeed in every endeavor!**

God-Power Within

"O the depth of the riches both of the wisdom and knowledge of God! How unsearchable are His judgements, and His ways past finding out!"

Romans 11:33 KJV

Last week we considered goals that were long range—what do I do with my life? Now it's time to become more specific. What short-range goals could you set? Remember, they should still be big enough to include God, but they should be specific enough for you to be able to reach them by the end of this week. Take the time to stop and think, and then write down one or two big goals you could reach this week:

By the end of this week, I _____

_____

_____

_____

_____

_____

_____

Now that you have stated your goals, is it big enough that you need God's help? I hope so! Spend some time today talking with God, asking Him for help, for inspiration, for courage, and for a plan to reach that goal.

> Today, I begin a new venture. Trusting God for the strength, the courage, the inspiration, the help I need to reach my goal!

God-Power Within

"For the Holy Spirit, God's gift, does not want you to be afraid of people, but to be wise and strong, and to love them and enjoy being with them."

2 Timothy 1:7

Ralph Johnson Bunche is a well-known American statesman. In 1950 Mr. Bunche won the Nobel peace prize, the first awarded to a Black. What was the secret of his climb to national and international success and acclaim?

He was born in Detroit, Michigan. His mother died when he was very young. His father, a butcher, supported the family until his death soon thereafter. Ralph Bunche was left an orphan at the age of twelve.

When his parents died, Ralph left Michigan and came to Los Angeles to live with his grandmother, Lucy Johnson. She was such an inspiring woman that near the end of her life, her writings were put into a limited publication entitled, "Believe in Yourself." I want to share with you something from that book.

In the first chapter she says, "Believe in yourself. Never say I am going to try, but, rather, I am going to do." There is sound advice in those two sentences. They hold the seed of self-confidence. And that trait is one God wants you to have.

Mrs. Johnson continues, "You must not only believe in yourself, you must believe in other people, too." Faith is not just directed towards God, but in successful people, faith is also directed to other people. She notes how often faith is emphasized in the Bible, "Read the Bible," she added, "and control your destiny!"

Small wonder that Ralph Bunche attained such distinction. He had Lucy Johnson and the example of her faith in Jesus Christ!

> **I feel the reservoir of God's strength welling up within me!**

God-Power Within

"And when I am lifted up [on the cross], I will draw every-one to me."

John 12:32

Jesus had a plan. He would bring salvation through the demonstration of unblemished love. If He could demonstrate that He could love the most unlovely soul, He could show us how salvation is possible. He could help us believe that God could forgive us in spite of ourselves. The cross was part of His plan. It took Jesus three years to accomplish His objective. But it was all according to plan. And if you want to reach your objective, you need a detailed plan on how to accomplish it. If you fail to plan, you are planning to fail!

What are your plans for reaching your objective this week? Write it out step-by-step:

Step 1. _____

_____

Step 2. _____

_____

Step 3. _____

_____

Step 4. _____

_____

Now go out and work your plan!

> **I plan to win! And with God's help,
> I will reach my goal!**

God-Power Within

"If I ride the morning winds to the farthest oceans, even theere your hand will guide me."

Psalm 139:9

Joe Frazier, former world heavyweight boxing champion, is a good example of Christian dreaming and planning. He is a dedicated Christian who reads his Bible nightly and goes to church regularly. He credits his success to faith in God.

As a young boy, Joe dreamed of becoming a boxer. He was inspired by Archie Moore, one of the greatest boxers of our time. Archie Moore, had a program called "ABC— Any Boy Can." That program inspired Joe Frazier to start.

He had no money, so he had to improvise. He got an old sack and filled it with sand and had a punching bag. That was the beginning of a dedicated, disciplined plan which ultimately led to Frazier's becoming the United States boxing representative for the Olympic games held in Tokyo in 1964.

He worked hard, prayed and believed. And even with a broken thumb, Frazier won the gold medal. He firmly believes that success depends on your road work. I agree. You must be willing to do your road work—month after month, year after year, hurdle after hurdle. That's called working your plan!

Frazier admits that many times he wanted to stop midway in his daily eight mile runs. He knew that no one would know the difference. But then he realized that he would only be fooling himself and that is the last person you want to deceive. Therefore he kept on running!

Whatever hurdles you face, keep on running! Dream— plan—succeed!

> **My future is bright.**
> **My God-inspired plan is working!**

God-Power Within

"My nourishment comes from doing the will of God who sent me, and from finishing his work.

John 4:34

Jesus had a constant burning desire to reach his objective. At the age of twelve, in the temple, He was about His father's business. Nothing could turn Him from His path.

Pat Nordberg is driven by the same kind of burning desire. For hours her life hung by a thread in surgery. Miraculously, she survived. But as a result of the surgery, she was left an aphasic. She had a partial loss of her ability to speak along with the loss of her memory for words.

She was faced with enormous problems to work out and overcome. In her aphasic condition, she began helping as a volunteer with mentally retarded children. This work inspired her with a dream—she would become a counselor and psychologist, specializing in working with mentally retarded children.

She dared to believe that with Christ she could do it. She started with a detailed plan. She figured that she would have to regain her muscle coordination, so she spent two years taking Hawaiian dancing lessons. She built up her strength to the point where she could take her driving test and get her license—step two. Now she was ready to tackle college.

Today, Pat has her degree. Her dream became a burning desire. She succeeded. Today she counsels with parents of aphasic children. Great things occur when you plan your course step-by-step!

> **God's power within me gives me strength. I am reaching my goal!**

God-Power Within

"He calms the storm and stills the waves."

Psalm 107:29

Earlier this week you set some short-range goals. Now it's time to evaluate your progress. How are you doing? Did you arrive at your objective? Did you get partway there? Describe how you feel you did:

_____

_____

_____

If you didn't reach your goal, it's time to restate your goal for next week. Don't let the seeds of discouragement defeat you just as you're beginning to succeed! If you did reach your goal, it's time to make some new ones for next week. Use your faith, and the power of God within to reach far. Stretch your faith. Remember, *Beginning is half-done!*

My new goals for this next week are:

1. _____

_____

2. _____

_____

3. _____

_____

> **I am anticipating success. My path is clear. Step-by-step God is giving me the power to reach my objectives!**

Enthusiasm For Today

"As for me and my family, we will serve the Lord."
Joshua 24:15

Dr. Norman Vincent Peale once asked a surgeon, "What's the most exciting operation you have ever performed in your career?" The doctor thought a brief moment and replied, "You know, of all the surgeries I have performed, there is one that stands out. It changed my life.

"There was this little girl with only a ten percent chance that she could survive. When I went into the operating room, there she was, a tiny little thing under the sheet, ashen grey face—so frail, so weak and helpless.

"Just as the nurses were going to prepare her for the anesthesia, I walked up to her and she looked at me and said, 'May I say something, doctor?' I said, 'Sure, honey.' 'Well, doctor,' she enthused, 'every night before I go to sleep I always pray a prayer. May I pray now?' I said, 'Of course.'

"Now I was having troubles of my own at that time with my son," the doctor continued, "and I was a very unhappy person. I stood there and told her to go ahead and pray, and to remember her doctor, too.

"She prayed, 'Jesus, tender shepherd, hear me. Watch your little lamb tonight . . . And Jesus, bless the doctor, too, because he's got troubles, too.' That broke me up, the doctor said. I turned away from the operating table so the nurses wouldn't see my tears. I prayed like I never prayed before, 'Oh God, if you ever use me to save a life, use me now to save this little girl!' She survived surgery and I found Jesus!"

> I feel Your spirit within me, Lord!
> What an enthusiastic life
> You are giving me!

Enthusiasm For Today

"And let us not get tired of doing what is right, for after a while we will reap a harvest of blessing."

Galatians 6:9

JESUS CHRIST IS ALIVE! And He gives you and me enthusiasm for today!

When you think about yourself;
Trouble grows.

When you think about Christ;
Trouble goes!

The exciting good news is that because Jesus Christ is alive, he has liberated Himself so that through the power of the Holy Spirit He can return again to live in your life and in my life! He cares about what is happening in your work, your dreams, your marriage and your family!

What can Jesus Christ do for you? I submit He can do for you what He is doing for me. He can reach you wherever you are; He can redeem you no matter how trapped you feel; he can unlock your possibilities and assure you of your worth—of the meaning and purpose of your life!

When you respond to His reach and let Him come into your life, you'll discover real enthusiasm for living! You will enjoy a better life, a happier life, a fuller life. He can reach you wherever you are!

Jesus Christ is reaching out to me!
He is changing my life. My heart is
overflowing with His confidence
and enthusiasm!

Enthusiasm For Today

"Once you knew very little of God's kindness; now your very lives have been changed by it."

1 Peter 2:10

As Peter wrote his first letter, he was enthused! He probably paused as he was writing and pictured in his mind the different people who would be reading his letter. And he was excited because their lives were changing! They were growing!

Think how your life has been changing as you daily discover more and more of God's kindness. List some of the changes taking place in your life:

Now that Jesus is in my life, I am becoming:

_____

_____

_____

_____

_____

_____

_____

You should be able to fill all the lines above, not because you have reached perfection, but because Jesus Christ has reached you and is giving you a real enthusiasm for living. Stop now and thank Him for all the good things He is doing in your life.

> **I am changing! I am in the process of becoming an even better person. Jesus Christ is alive and involved in my life!**

Enthusiasm For Today

"I know that I shall again have plenty of reason to praise Him for all that He will do. He is my help! He is my God!"
Psalm 42:11

He had no religion, never did have, according to his testimony to me later. But that morning he flipped the TV dial trying to check the weather, and for a moment watched this minister from Los Angeles being interviewed on a talk show. He listened a bit, then continued his search for news of the weather, and then turned off the set.

Later that morning, he couldn't get that minister out of his mind. All he could remember was the fact that he was speaking that night at the Hilton Hotel. He couldn't get his mind off those few minutes that morning on TV.

Finally he called the Hilton in San Francisco. Yes, there was a convention. Yes, there was a Dr. Schuller speaking. No, he could not get a ticket, it was a closed meeting.

Undaunted, the man got into his car, drove to San Francisco and went to the meeting. When he arrived, the usher was not at the door. He walked in and sat down in the back. He heard me say, "God is reaching out to you. A hundred times each day God reaches out to you but you don't recognize that it is God. He wants you to know that you need forgiveness. God reaches out to you to redeem you so you can discover the enthusiasm He gives for living!

Suddenly, that young man said in his heart, "Jesus I want you to come into my life." And just as suddenly, God reached down and filled him with joy, confidence and enthusiasm. He was redeemed!

> **God is filling me with His joy, His confidence and His enthusiasm. I am redeemed! I am a child of God!**

Enthusiasm For Today

"And you should follow my example, just as I follow Christ's."

1 Corinthians 11:1

Enthusiasm is contagious—especially when its source is Jesus Christ! My enthusiasm was transmitted through a TV set and into the mind of a man who searched until he found where I was speaking. God used that instance to draw that man to Himself.

Saint Paul was so enthusiastic about Jesus Christ that he wrote to the believers in Corinth and said, "Follow me just as I follow Christ!" That's enthusiasm!

Who are the enthusiastic people in your life? Which fellow-Christians inspire you by their enthusiasm and faith? Write their names below along with a brief description of the attractiveness of their enthusiasm.

| | THEIR ENTHUSIASM |
NAME	INSPIRES ME BECAUSE

My enthusiasm is growing. I can feel joy within me as I begin this day.

Enthusiasm For Today

*"And I am sure that God who began the good work within
you will keep right on helping you grow in his grace."*
                                        Philippians 1:6

Michelangelo is credited with forty-four statues created
in his lifetime, but he only finished fourteen of them.
Now you are familiar with the fourteen he finished—
David, the Pieta, and Moses, to mention a few.

But the thirty he never finished are very interesting. I
have seen many of them . . . a huge chunk of marble and
out of it is sculptured an elbow or the beginning of a wrist.
The rest of the human form is still locked up in the marble.

Another chunk shows a leg, with the thigh, knee, calf,
heel and foot clearly chiseled out of the hard stone, but the
rest of the body is still locked within. And then another
one shows the head and shoulders of a man, but the rest
of the body is still frozen inside.

When I saw these unfinished masterpieces in a museum
in Italy, the thought struck me, "Of all the tragedies in life,
the greatest tragedy is for a person to live and die and
never be told what his possibilities are." And then I
thought of the possibilities still locked within me and my
enthusiasm for God's releasing power grew. Jesus Christ
reaches us so that He can redeem us and release our possibilities!

You are an unfolding masterpiece in the hands of God—
the master sculptor!

**I am unfolding. Today I can already
see new possibilities emerging.
God is at work in my life!**

Enthusiasm For Today

O God, when a life has been so richly blessed as mine has
been, it is not right for me to be laughing! I confess that I
am responsible for my moods. I have no right to selfishly
indulge in negative feelings of self-pity. It's time for me to
change my mental dial, Lord.

You are helping me.
This will be the moment when the sun breaks through the
parted clouds, and the springtime returns after winter.

Thank you, Lord! The dreary, depressing, disconsolate
mood disappears like the morning mist in the glowing
sunshine of your love.

And joy moves in!
And hope begins to build up within me!
And a beautiful feeling of enthusiasm starts to surround
me!

Thank you, God, for the great things you are doing within
me now in this moment of prayer.

Amen.

Never Be Afraid

"And the one who comes to me I will never turn away."
                                        John 6:37 NEB

It happened one night in France. There was a Halloween party and a hundred happy young people were having a ball. Somehow a fire started—no one ever knew how. People ran but were unable to find the exits. Most of them died.

In that hall there were doors built for one purpose and one purpose only—namely, to get out in time of danger. But these doors were unseen. They were covered with curtains.

Early the next morning as firemen checked through the burned out building, they pulled what was left of the curtains aside and found the doors. *But the doors had been nailed shut to prevent party crashers.* And the result was people perished!

Somebody dreamed of a building, and they planned a safety door.

. . . some were afraid of it and hammered it shut!

Jesus Christ is God's plan to be the door,
    the door through which you can enter
    into a closeness with God
        into salvation
        into eternal life,
into a life where there is no fear at all!

"I am the door!
    Don't hammer me shut! Open me! Walk through!
    I will never forget your name!
    I will never forget your face!
    You are mine!"

Never Be Afraid

"Don't be afraid, for I have ransomed you;
I have called you by name; you are mine.
  When you go through deep waters
  and great trouble,
    I WILL BE WITH YOU.
When you go through rivers of difficulty,
you wil not drown!
When you walk through the fire of oppression,
you will not be burned up—
  the flames will not consume you

For I am the Lord your God, your Savior . . .
  you are precious to me and honored,
  and I love you.

Don't be afraid, for I am with you.

Isaiah 43:1-5

Never Be Afraid

"Cheer up! Take courage if your are depending on the Lord."

Psalm 31:24

Courage belongs to those who depend on the Lord, says the psalmist. And I say we need to continually affirm our dependence on his power to protect us. Today we're going to create a litany which affirms our faith in God's power so that we need never be afraid. In the blank spaces, write down some situation that strikes fear in your heart. When you have finished, read your litany of courage and praise. You need, never be afraid!

When I _____
   I will put my trust in God.

When I _____
   The Lord gives me courage!

When I _____
   The Lord is my light and salvation!

When I _____
   My heart shall know no fear! God will save me!

When I _____
   God will send the help I need!

When I _____
   I am expecting the Lord to rescue me!

When I _____

> **I am brave, stouthearted and courageous, for the Lord is with me and helps me!**

Never Be Afraid

"In my troubles I pled with God to help me and He did!"
Psalm 120:1

Imagine for a moment that you are lined up along a street waiting for a parade. It has been said that Jesus Christ is going to pass by.

As he comes down the street, you can hear the applause. Most of us, perhaps all of us, would applaud Him.

"That is Christ."

"He is wonderful."

"Isn't He great?"

But watch! From time to time, there are those who do not applaud. They break through the rope, dash into the middle of the street, and for a moment take hold of His hand . . .

Jesus looks at them,

faces close—

Something happens between them and then they slip back and once more stand at the curb. But they are changed. And the biggest change of all is a boldness, a fearlessness, and recklessness that transforms them into exciting, enthused, world-changers!

Each of us must do the same thing. It is not enough just to applaud, to admire, to respect, to adore, or even to worship. We must break out and take hold of His hand for a moment! And as he looks at us, our fears will vanish! We know Him—the creator of the universe. And He knows us!

> My fears are slipping away.
> I can feel my courage growing as I
> reach out to God. He comes to me and
> knows who I am!

Never Be Afraid

*"Stand up and praise the Lord your God, for He lives from
everlasting to everlasting. Praise His glorious name!"*
                                                    Nehemiah 9:5

The people who live next door to us have three
Doberman Pinschers. The huge dogs welcomed us soon
after we moved in. They are marvelous beautiful creatures,
but ferocious. I still keep at least ten feet between me and
the fence. When I do my running they see me, and as soon
as I make the curve near their yard they come racing after
me, teeth bared, foaming at the mouth. I'm alive because
of the fence!

My little girl, though, walks through their yard and
plays with the little neighbor girl, and the Dobermans
never bother her. I keep saying, "Honey, you'd better
watch out for those big dogs." And she answers, "Daddy,
those dogs are trained." I reply, "I know they're trained,
but be careful!" But she persists, "Daddy, you just don't
understand. Those dogs are trained only to bite somebody
who is running. That's why they never bite me or
Gretchen!"

Now I've never experimented with that theory, but I do
know this. After all my years as a pastor, I can confidently
say that most, if not all of our fears are the kind that are
trained to strike at our hearts only when we run away from
them. Face them, and we find they are not enemies at all.
They are a shadow in our path—it's that simple! Face your
fears and they fade away!

> I can live bravely and love dangerously
> for God is with me!

Never Be Afraid

"Don't be afraid. Just stand where you are and watch, and you will see the wonderful way the Lord will rescue you today."

Exodus 14:13

A couple of days ago you created a litany of praise affirming your confidence in God's power. In that litany, you listed several things that create fear within you. Go back to that list and choose one of those fears that you might have to face today. Describe it:

_____

_____

_____

Today, instead of running, or reacting, or hiding, you are going to FACE YOUR FEAR! Stop! turn around and look your fear in the eye. Now write down three positive steps you are going to take today to face this fear and conquer it. As you do, claim the promise in Exodus 14:13, for God will be with you!

1. _____

_____

2. _____

_____

3. _____

_____

> **I am not afraid. God is with me and together we are invincible!**

Never Be Afraid

"The Lord will fight for you, and you won't need to lift a finger!"

Exodus 14:14

I love the story about old Doctor John McNeil, who was a famous American preacher some years ago. He said, "When I was a lad in Scotland I used to work late and in order to get home I had to walk a long distance. I had to go several miles through a little village and then through a narrow canyon where criminals and thieves were known to hide.

"This particular Saturday night I walked as fast as I could. My heart was pounding in my teenage chest, for the night was as black as a wolf's jaw. Not a star was shining. The moon was dark. There were no lights in the sky.

"I rounded a bend of the road in the most desolate, the most forsaken and the most frightening part of the whole canyon. Suddenly, there was a call in the night! For a moment my heart stopped. The call came again, and it was my father's voice. He was coming out to meet me at the worst part of the canyon. 'John! It's your dad!' he said.

"In a moment his large hand was on my shoulder and his heavy feet were falling at my side. I was home right then and there!"

You are always home when your Father comes to meet you. For God has promised, "I will be with you!" He knows you. He calls you. And He is with you! You need never be afraid again!

Your quiet and calming spirit is flowing within me now, Lord. My fear is gone!

Tranquilize Tension

"For God is not a God of confusion but of peace."
                              1 Corinthians 14:33 RSV

"Relax, Dr. Schuller, just relax," my golf instructor told me. "Why, I'm quite relaxed," I assured him as I gripped my club fiercely, as if it were a sword.

"Feel the muscles in the back of your legs," my teacher continued, adding, "I dare say that every muscle in your body is tense right now. I can see it—even your cheek and lip muscles are tensed up! You've got to relax!"

I waited and he kept right on preaching to me. "All right, Dr. Schuller, mentally unwind. Loosen up the muscles on your forehead. Now relax your eyebrows, now your cheeks, now your tongue and your mouth. Now your whole face. Good!" he added as encouragement. "Now keep on relaxing your muscles across your shoulders. Feel the soothing, balmy relaxation flow like warm water over your whole body. Let the tension drip away. Now breathe deeply and exhale slowly. Do it again."

It all sounded silly, but as he repeated this process and I agreed to do what he suggested, it really worked! I relaxed so much the golf club fell out of my hand!

Well, I never learned to play golf very well but those lessons did make me aware of tension I never sensed before. And only as we become sensitive to the presence of tension will we begin to do something about it!

God didn't create us for tension. Instead, He has provided us with tension tranquilizers. And He is the source of all tranquility!

**I feel tension dripping away as I
fill my thoughts with Jesus!**

Tranquilize Tension

*"I will lie down in peace and sleep, for though I am alone,
O Lord, you will keep me safe."*

Psalm 4:8

Now, before we can attempt to
    Paralyze the destructive effect, or
    Sterilize the reproductive effect, or
    Tranquilize the seductive effect of tension, let's
Sensitize ourselves to the reality of tension, and
Analyze what gets us uptight in the first place:

I GET TENSE AND UPTIGHT WHEN

1. _____

2. _____

3. _____

4. _____

5. _____

THE MAIN CAUSE OF MY TENSION IS

_____

_____

I feel my tension and I choose instead
to look to Jesus Christ, the source of
peace and tranquility!

Tranquilize Tension

"I am leaving you with a gift—peace of mind and heart!"
John 14:27

In my world travels, I have run across all kinds of trinkets, tricks and techniques for relieving tension—everything from "worry beads" to a rubbing stone. But I find nothing that can compare with the peace that Jesus Christ brings into the human heart.

Gilbert Chesterton, after wandering far and wide in his lifetime of free thinking, came back at last to faith. He said, "It was like a man setting sail from England to discover some great new land. Into the fog he sailed, for days and days—confident that he would make some great new discovery.

"Finally, as the fog lifted he saw land, and coming to this exotic shore he ran up and down the beach. He hoisted the English flag with dreams of naming this new land after himself. But in his running across the beach, he turned a bend and noted, with shock and dismay this was only the other side of Britain. Trying to escape England—he came back to England."

Trying to turn away from Christ, through centuries and cultures man can only come back to Him again and again! For only Jesus Christ can bring true tranquility.

Lord, I turn to You and feel the warm rays of Your love filling me with peace of mind and heart! Thank you!

Tranquilize Tension

Sunshine after rain,
Dewdrops on a rose,
A baby sleeping sweetly in the crib,
A bird drinking from a fountain,
A leaf floating on quiet water, and
A mind focused on God;

Such is the peace I feel
deep within my being
now
as
I close my eyes and think about Jesus Christ.

Thank you, God.
Amen.

Tranquilize Tension

"His peace will keep your thoughts and your hearts quiet and at rest as you trust in Christ Jesus."

Philippians 4:7

God's first tension tranquilizer is FREEDOM. Nothing tranquilizes like real freedom—shoes off, running barefoot on the windy and sandy beach, alive and free!

But real freedom is found in the commitment of responsible inter-personal relationships. We often think of freedom as *total freedom*—freedom without responsibility. That's the kind of freedom the prodigal son experienced, and the end of that road is utter loneliness and despair.

Real freedom comes within a relationship, like the relaxing freedom that comes the moment you run into the arms of a caring, loving God. At that point you can say good-bye to the "I'm trapped" tensions; the "I'm boxed-in" tensions; the "I'm stuck-in-a-rut" tensions.

Have you experienced real freedom? Describe a time recently when you experienced this kind of freedom and write down what that freedom felt like: _____

_____

_____

_____

God, I run to Your arms. As You lovingly care for me I experience the joy of real freedom—the freedom to become!

Tranquilize Tension

"So now, since we have been made right in God's sight . . .
we can have real peace with him because of what Jesus
Christ our Lord has done for us."

Romans 5:1

Forgiveness—God's healing tranquilizer number two!

Forgiveness is the flow of divine love through your spiritual consciousness. It is God, real and alive; A Powerful Positive Emotion flowing through you. Deep Peace and Power surge instantaneously through your soul.

Tensions flow out when you take and give forgiveness.

Dectection tension—"what if they find out?"

Exposure tension—"what if people tell on me?"

These terrible tensions are gone when you experience God's forgiveness.

Hostility Tension, Anger Tension, Resentment Tension, Retaliation Tension—all these leave you as you begin to practice forgiveness. Here is a tranquilizer that really tranquilizes!

HE WHO FORGIVES ENDS THE TENSION!

All sorts of mental battles cease at the peace table of Divine Forgiveness. Who do you need to meet at that table? God? A parent? A child? A friend? A co-worker? Stop now and in your mind visualize a table—a Divine Forgiveness Table. And seated at that table is you—and God—and _____ . And as God forgives you, your heart is filled with forgiveness towards that other person. "Forgive us our sins, just as we have forgiven those who have sinned against us." (Matthew 6:12).

I am filled with forgiveness.
I hold no grudges. God's tranquilizer
of forgiveness fills me with peace!

Tranquilize Tension

"For Christ himself is our way of peace. He has made peace between us . . . by making us all one family."

Ephesians 2:14

Freedom, Forgiveness and FELLOWSHIP are the three sacred tranquilizers that really tranquilize. Fellowship is that deep, serene, trusting experience that is available between you and God, and between you and your fellow man.

Fellowship with God—Divine Fellowship—how easy it is to empty the cup of this relaxing drink! How it relieves. Suddenly loneliness tension and rejection tension are gone. When we experience acceptance by God and enjoy fellowship with Him, faith, hope and love flood our being. All tension is gone!

When we experience fellowship with God we also desire fellowship with the family of God. And in that fellowship together, we can experience the healing power of God's Spirit working. For in the fellowship of the family of God, we discover that we are not alone, our troubles are not unique, our hurdles can be conquered!

It's time to come to the party. When the prodigal returned home, he tasted all three tranquilizers. The tranquilizer of fellowship was the party in the house. Your tensions will vanish as you come inside to the party and enjoy the fellowship of the Family of God!

Tension is gone! I experience the
tranquilizers of freedom, forgiveness
and fellowship!

Liberate Your Imagination

"So God made man like his Maker. Like God did God make man."

Genesis 1:27

It's exciting to me to realize that I am made in the image of God. What does that mean to you? To me, the image of God means that I share with Him His most distinctive qualities—including His Creative Power! God is Creative! He is Cosmic Imagination! When you look at the splendor of God's creation, you know that one of the primary features of His image is His Creativity!

Only human beings share the gift of creative imagination with God. You have it. I have it. But for many of us our imagination is locked up in a cage. And we cannot become the person we might dare to dream we could become until our imaginations are liberated!

I remember listening to one of the American POW's who had just returned from Vietnam. He had been held captive by the Vietcong in a tiger cage. These cages were made of bamboo, and were about six feet long, four feet high and two feet wide.

This man told how one night he managed to work one of the bamboo rods loose. Soon he had another one loose and then another, until finally he slipped out of the cage and made his escape. As I listened to him, I thought of the mental tiger cages that holds our creativity captive. Our potentially powerful imagination is imprisoned in a tiger cage of our own mind!

It's time to liberate your imagination and discover the dreams God has for your life!

> I am made in the image of God! I share His creative power. He is at work helping me liberate my imagination!

Liberate Your Imagination

"For God is at work in you, both to will and to work for his good pleasure."

Philippians 2:13 RSV

There are five bars in our mental tiger cages that must be loosened. Let's look at them this week.

First, our *frights* restrict our imagination. Nothing holds people back more than the fear of failure. And no fright more than this one keeps us from really imagining the person we could become.

Is there a fear within you today? What is it? _____

_____

2 Timothy 1:7 says, "God has not given us the spirit of fear." (KJV). So it is possible for us to overcome our fears! We overcome our fears when we realize that our fears do not come from God and hence are not to be trusted!

Don't surrender your life and your future to fear. In the name of Christ, command any fears to *get out!* Work your imagination free from imprisoning and unreliable fears by first of all recognizing that God is at work within you for good. Then boldly repeat out loud this affirmation:

> **In the name of Jesus Christ, I command my fear to get out of me, to release my mind and depart forever!**

Liberate Your Imagination

"For God, who said, 'Let there be light in the darkness,' has made us understand that it is the brightness of his glory that is seen in the face of Jesus Christ."

2 Corinthians 4:6

The second bar in our mental tiger cage is our *nights*. I'm thinking about the dark times of life; the experiences that hurt us. Both our *frights* and our *nights* can bind our imagination.

I met a man on the way to the airport in North Carolina. He was filled with enthusiasm. He said, "Dr. Schuller, you would never have known me a couple of years ago. Christ has transformed my life!"

He went on to tell me how be had been raised on a farm outside of Charlotte. As a young man he said, "There must be a better life than this." The work was hard and one could barely make a living farming. "I borrowed all I could," he said, "and set up a business selling farm machinery. Four farm machinery businesses went bankrupt that year and I was one of them. I was penniless: no trade or skill except farming, and I wasn't ready to go back to farming."

"What happened?" I asked. "Well, I took a job in a post office doing menial work. But I felt trapped. I was so depressed I would often go into the rest room and bawl like a baby. This went on for eight years!

"One day a fellow came into the post office and asked me why he never saw me smile. He told me, 'You *can* smile, for God loves you!' That man introduced me to Jesus Christ and gave me the courage to start another business. My dark night is over!" he affirmed.

> **I stand boldly in the dark, for Jesus is with me. He gives me freedom!**

Liberate Your Imagination

"For you are all children of the light and of the day, and do not belong to darkness and night."

1 Thessalonians 5:5

What experiences in your past are holding you back? Is it a setback, a hurt, a failure, a defeat, a reverse, a rejection? Refuse to surrender leadership of your future life to past hurts! If you're afraid of getting hurt again, you'll never break free.

Stop a moment today and write down one or two experiences in your past that could be called "night" experiences:

_____

_____

_____

Now look at those experiences carefully and positively. What "good" things were you able to learn from those experiences?

_____

_____

_____

_____

Now affirm that you are a child of the day—darkness and night are no longer a part of you!

> The past is past. I am alive today and living in the light. I am filled with possibilities for today!

Liberate Your Imagination

"Jesus said to the people, 'I am the Light of the world. So if you follow me, you won't be stumbling through the darkness, for living light will flood your path.' "

John 8:12

The third rod that binds our imagination in mental tiger cages is the *light*. How can that be, you ask? How can success bind us?

It's easy to see how some people can be restricted from becoming the great people they should become by the hurts of life, but it is just as true that some people are bound by the highlights of life.

SUCCESS IS NEVER SETTLED!

That means there are always greater things that you can and should do. If you attain a goal, and become so enamored with the glory and the honor and the laurels that you stay there—then your imagination is being darkened and bound by the lights, by the success in your life. Don't be blinded by light!

Some people come to Jesus and accept His light in their life. But then they stop there. Their growth is blocked; their imagination is locked in a cage; they are bound by the light!

But the light of Jesus is meant to show us the path to greater possibilities and richer experiences. When you are tempted to stop along the path of life and enjoy the view, resist that urge. Step forward and move onward to new and greater heights. Don't let the light of your victories cause you to become a failure.

> I am walking in the light today.
> I resist the urge to stand still— I move
> forward and onward with Jesus!

Liberate Your Imagination

"Be honest in your estimate of yourselves, measuring your value by how much faith God has given you."

Romans 12:3

The fourth rod in our mental tiger cage is our *blights*. I don't think anything keeps people from becoming the people God wants them to be more than perfectionism.

Consider the limiting, lowering, negative influence of these statements: "I can't do it." "I'm not as good as others." "I'm not beautiful." "I'm not smart."

What's your favorite excuse? Write it down:

_____

My publisher challenged me once with this point: "Dr. Schuller," he said, "you've got to prove to people that it's not talent that makes them reach the top." "But talent is terribly important," I argued, "After all, I can be a possibility thinker, but I can't sing like Beverly Sills."

He insisted, "You do somemore research, Schuller!" And I did. And I discovered that in every profession you will find that the people at the top are not the most talented people in their professions. *The people at the top have learned to ignore their blights!*

Time to rewrite the sentence above. Or better yet, write a new sentence that affirms the great, unlimited potential God has placed within your life!

_____

_____

Liberate Your Imagination

"I am still not at all I should be but I am bringing all my energies to bear on this one thing: . . . I strain to . . . receive the prize."

Philippians 3:13, 14

The fifth rod in our mental cage—our *sights*. They are too low or too short. We don't think long enough or far enough. Just because we can't reach our objective in five months doesn't mean we can't do it in the next five years.

One of my favorite stories is about the man fishing off a pier. He would catch a fish, measure it, and if it was ten inches or less, he would throw it in the bucket. If the fish he caught was over ten inches, he threw it back!

Another person, observing this ritual, thought the fisherman was crazy. Finally he asked, "Why do you throw the big ones away and keep the little fish?"

The fisherman answered, "My frying pan is only ten inches!"

Now you may laugh at that, but the news I have for you is this: You and I are that fisherman! The big ideas God sends our way are tossed out. We only keep the smaller ones.

As you liberate your imagination, God is going to stretch your dreams and your thinking. Remember, God loves everyone of us, but He is not satisfied with any one of us!

My prayer is this, "Dear God, help me to catch the dream of the person you want me to be! Even if it's bigger than I've ever imagined before. And, God, don't let me be so scared that I try to throw your dream back!"

> Glory hallelujah! I feel it
> coming on. Make me ready for a
> brand new start today, Lord!

Winning Is Beginning

"Behold, now is the acceptable time; behold, now is the day of salvation."

2 Corinthians 6:2 RSV

To really succeed in life, all you have to do is to solve two problems. (1) *Get started!* (2) *Never quit!* these two problems are the only ones you need to solve to become the person God wants you to be!

You didn't think when you got up this morning that this would be the day your life would change, did you? But it's going to happen! Because the only thing that stands between you and grand success in living are these two problems—getting started and never quitting! You can solve your biggest problem. You can get started right here and now.

I don't know what idea is in your mind right now, but I know that everyone has within themselves some idea of something that he or she should be starting and hasn't. Maybe it's to lose weight. Maybe it's to get started on an exercise program. Maybe it's to join the church. Maybe it's to accept Jesus Christ as your Savior and Lord. Maybe it's to read the Bible. Or maybe it's to start a new business.

Now—what will you do with that idea? Whatever you do, don't waste it! And you keep from wasting it by beginning to *do* something about it!

Maybe you just need to write down your idea: _____

_____

_____

My decision today will become tomorrow's reality! I treat every new idea with great care!

Winning Is Beginning

"Then the Lord said to Moses, 'Quit praying and get the people moving!' "

Exodus 14:15

I remember visiting Hope College, in Holland, Michigan, while my son was a student there studying for the ministry. He's a great young man, the only son I have, and I'm very proud of him.

Bob and I walked around the campus, our arms around each other's shoulders, and I said to him, "Bob, do you know the most important thing I learned on this campus? I don't think it was Greek or Hebrew. I don't think it was History or Psychology. The most important thing I learned while a student on this campus I learned right there in that room." And I pointed to the room where I took History 101.

"The coach was the professor," I continued. "One day in the middle of the semester he asked, 'How many of you students have started your term paper?' And not a hand went up. I've never forgotten what happened because I am indebted to him—and so are you," I enthused to Bob. "He paced up and down across the front of the classroom— just like a coach. He didn't say a thing, but everyone knew something was coming. He was getting ready!

"Finally he stopped, turned and faced the class. In a loud voice he said, 'I don't care if you all flunk this course and forget everything you have ever learned on this campus. But don't *ever* forget the sentence I'm about to say to you now.' Then he paused and bellowed it out:

" 'BEGINNING IS HALF DONE!' "

> Today, with God's help, I begin
> that project I've been putting off!

Winning Is Beginning

"Hard work means prosperity; only a fool idles away his time."

Proverbs 12:11

Often we hear the question: How do you treat people? A far more important question is: *How do you treat ideas?*

Treat them tenderly . . .
  They can be killed quickly.
Treat them gently . . . .
  They can be bruised in infancy.
Treat them respectfully . . .
  They could be the most valuable thing that ever came into your life.
Treat them protectively . . .
  Don't let them get away.
Treat them nutritionally . . .
  Feed them and feed them well.
Treat them antiseptically . . .
  Don't let them get infected with the germs of negative thoughts.
Treat them responsibly!
  Respond! Act! Do something with them!
DECIDE TO DECIDE!

I treat each idea as a gift from God's hand. They are a sacred responsibility to me!

Winning Is Beginning

"Never be lazy in your work but serve the Lord enthusiastically."

Romans 12:11

Go back to the 24th and look at the idea you wrote down. Are you still excited? Then let's get started! Set up a file; start a notebook; open a special account; but *do* something!

I remembered a teacher's negative remark to me when I was faced with writing my first book. She had said, "Bob Schuller, I think you can make a living talking, but don't ever try to write." But as the negative thoughts that surrounded her comment moved through my mind, I also remembered that "Beginning is half done." So I took out a piece of paper and typed the title of my book on it. I bought a loose-leaf binder, and stuck the title sheet in it. And before I knew it, I had written a book!

What can you do *today* to begin? Write it down:

_____

_____

_____

_____

What can you do this week to keep moving on your idea?

_____

_____

> Now that I've started, I'm half done.
> And I can feel enthusiasm building
> within me. I know I can finish!

Winning Is Beginning

"This should be your ambition: to live a quiet life minding your own business and doing your own work."
                                    1 Thessalonians 4:11

When faced with a God-inspired idea, insecure people hibernate. They run away from good ideas. They're afraid they might fall or that it might cost too much. Like a bear feeling the first whisper of a winter wind, they rush off to hide.

Lazy people luxuriate. They just don't pay much attention to the idea. They just want to enjoy the pleasures of the moment. They say they'll get serious later on, but seldom do anything different.

Wounded people commiserate. They say, "Oh, it's a good idea, but I couldn't do it. I've tried before and failed." They have a long list of "I've tried but . . ." excuses that seem endless.

Foolish people procrastinate. They put things off and say, "Later on when I'm ready. But I'm not ready yet." And the difference between the high achiever and the low achiever is that the high achiever almost always makes decisions before he's ready to move! Don't wait until you're ready or you'll never make the move.

Wise people dedicate themselves to the task and move in. They're do-it-now people. They don't waste a good moment or a good idea—especially when that idea comes from God.

Which kind of person will you be today?

Lord, I'm moving in and making the decision now to act on the idea You've given me. I feel Your strength and help as I act in faith!

Winning Is Beginning

"I can do everything God asks me to with the help of Christ who gives me the strength and power."

Philippians 4:13

I've learned one important thing about beginning. I can do anything I think I can . . . *but I can't do anything alone!* I've taught this, preached it, written it, tried it, and it's true. Always, I need someone to support me! Don't try to handle your dreams alone. It won't work.

Winning starts with beginning, and beginning starts when you get up and do something. And the exciting thing is God is there with you to give you the strength and the power you need!

Write a prayer of thanksgiving for his presence with you and affirm his help as you begin to act on your dream:

DEAR LORD, I THANK YOU FOR _____

_____

_____

_____

_____

_____ . AMEN.

> God is doing something beautiful in my heart this very moment. I sense a miracle is happening. Thank You!

Winning Is Beginning

TEN COMMANDMENTS FOR HANDLING GOD'S IDEAS

1. I will never vote no to any idea because "It's impossible."
2. I will never block a helpful thought because it entails problems, or wait to begin until I find solutions.
3. I will never oppose a possibility because I've never done it and can't imagine how it could be done.
4. I will never obstruct a plan because it runs a risk of failure.
5. I will never cooperate in defeating a potentially good idea because I can see something wrong with it.
6. I will never squelch a creative idea because no one else has ever succeeded in perfecting it.
7. I will never declare any constructive concept to be impossible because I lack the time, money, brains, energy, talent, or skill to exploit it.
8. I will never discard a plan or project just because it's imperfect.
9. I will never resist a proposal because I didn't think of it, won't get credit for it, won't personally benefit from it, or may not live to see and enjoy it.
10. I will never quit because I've reached the end of the rope, I will tie a knot and hang on!

Listen And Glisten

"Be still and know that I am God"

Psalm 46:10 RSV

When I was in high school I sang in a male quartet. Later, when I entered college, I made it a point of joining another quartet. We made many college concert tours across America. In fact, my first trip to California was with the Hope College traveling, touring quartet.

One of the things I will never forget is my high school music teacher saying, "Boys, the key to a good male quartet is equally balanced harmony. All voices must be balanced!" Then she went on to explain how to obtain harmony.

"Listen to yourself sing, but also listen to the other voices on each side of you," she explained. "If the voices on either side of you are a little louder than you, you know that you have to sing a little louder. If you hear yourself louder than you hear those on each side of you, then you are singing too loud—tone down a little. *All you have to do is use your ears!* Make sure you don't sing louder or softer than the voices around you. Learn to listen!"

I have discovered that this is also an important principle in all relationships in life. The tragedy is most people only listen to themselves and to their own will and desires. And that always produces disharmony. Listen—and you will find harmony!

**I relax, I still my mind, and I pray.
I listen with love!**

Listen And Glisten

"This is my Son, my Chosen One; listen to him."
Luke 9:35

Listen! The difference between people who are morbid, morose, melancholic and pessimistic, and those who sparkle, twinkle, are vibrant and alive is not genetic! It is mental. Glistening personalities are people who are listening. They listen to themselves, their family members, their friends and working companions, and to God Himself. And they glisten because their sensitive listening produces a deep inner harmony.

But the enthusiastic radiant person has also chosen to listen to the positive voices. They have developed the habit of turning off the negative sounds that vibrate through our society.

What are you listening to? Let's take an inventory of the past 24 hours:

POSITIVE VOICES	NEGATIVE VOICES

I am blocking out the negative voices around me and tuning in to all the positive resources God has for me!

Listen And Glisten

"Be still before the Lord, and wait patiently for him."
                                        Psalm 37:7 RSV

Henry Fawcett was one of the great distinguished members of Parliament in England. Gladstone appointed him Postmaster General, and he made some of the greatest contributions to England in the area of postal services and telegraphy.

The interesting fact behind Fawcett's success is this: *He was completely blind!* Here was a man who had every reason to be bitter. When he was 20 years old, he and his father were on a hunting trip. They enjoyed a very close relationship as father and son.

On this trip, the father accidently discharged his rifle and shot his son in the face. This bright, healthy, mentally alert young boy dropped in a pool of blood. The lad lived, but he was sightless the rest of his life.

The father wanted to kill himself. Young Henry wanted to die, too. He had no hope of reading or returning to his studies. All of these negative thoughts flooded his mind day after day.

One day, Henry overheard his father crying. His father was in deep despair. Henry decided to build his father's hopes by pretending, "It's okay, dad. Others can read to me, I'll make it!" He lived a lie of joy and happiness before his father, but then something happened. The lie became a reality! He had hope! His life had meaning! He was dynamically changed because he chose to listen to the positive, not the negative!

> **My thoughts are centered on positive voices. I can feel hope and joy within!**

Listen And Glisten

"Shine as lights in the (dark) world!"

Philippians 2:15 KJV

What kind of voice are you? Two days ago we did an inventory of the kind of voices you hear each day. Perhaps a more important question is: *Are you a positive or a negative voice to yourself and others?*

Describe an example of when you were a positive voice this week to someone else: _____

_____

_____

Now describe an example of when you were a negative voice this week to someone else: _____

_____

_____

Today, you can put a light in someone else's face! It is a decision you can make. If you will listen to God, who speaks to you through Jesus Christ, you can be a shining light in a dark world. *Determine now* to be a positive voice today to someone. As evidence of your commitment, write down their name:

_____

> God's thoughts are filling me. Today I share these positive thoughts with someone. I am God's light!

Listen And Glisten

"We will lovingly follow the truth at all times—speaking truly, dealing truly, living truly."

Ephesians 4:15

Several years ago, Mrs. Schuller and I celebrated our twenty-fifth wedding anniversary. Over twenty-five super years! And our marriage is better today than it was then and it keeps getting better everyday. Let me share our secret.

When we came to California, we recognized that we would be getting into a situation that would create many pressures. And we knew that the most important thing in our life was our marriage. So on a Monday night my wife and I had a date—and we reserved every Monday night for our "date-night" with each other.

And so every Monday for over twenty years, with rare exceptions, we have planned a special night to ourselves. And that meant that every seven days we would get our marriage, our thinking, *our listening*, and our communication lines clean and clear.

I compare it to the alignment of the wheels on my car. I am constantly bumping curbs or hitting ruts in the road. About every six months or so, someone will say, "Dr. Schuller, you need to get your front wheels aligned. You're wasting rubber."

Now if I went in every week to have my front wheels aligned, my front tires would last twice as long. (But it's cheaper to replace the tires.) I'll tell you something: My marriage and my family mean so much to me that every week my wife and I have a realignment scheduled. And the important thing is we listen to each other. As a result, we keep growing closer together!

Lord, I listen to You. Help me keep my alignment right as I live today!

Listen And Glisten

Too often, O God, the sacred calm
of your still small voice
is overpowered by
the roar of the traffic,
the moan of ambulances,
the wail of sirens,
the growl of buses,
the rude interruption of the doorbell.

Jet airplanes, trucks, trains, television, telephones fill my everyday world with noises my ears were never designed to tolerate.

An irritating assortment of unnatural sounds drown your silver-soft voice, Lord, which whispers through the trees. Oh, my Lord, there are birds winging and I do not see them, children playing and I do not hear them, flowers blooming and I do not enjoy them, clouds sailing silently through the soundless sea of space and I do not see them!

God, you are living and moving and I do not feel you! Increase my awareness of the throbbing reality of the dynamic spiritual universe around me, Lord.

God! You are moving in mighty thoughts and feelings within me now! I am surrounded with an awareness of you that gives me a new lease on life! Thank you, God! Amen.

Listen And Glisten

"How precious to me are thy thoughts, O God! How vast is the sum of them!"

Psalm 139:17 RSV

I talked with a father recently who has two daughters working in very influential positions in our nation's capitol. I said to him, "How did you ever manage to have two daughters in such powerful positions on Capitol Hill?"

"It wasn't easy for me, Dr. Schuller," he answered. "I used to take them to the capitol when they were little girls so they could see the seats of power. My one daughter graduated from high school and I wanted her to go to college. But she said, 'I'm going to get a job—I'm going to become a secretary to one of our great senators!' "

The father continued, "I didn't want to let her go. I didn't dare let her leave home and go out into that city without me or her mother!"

I asked him what made him give in and this is what he told me. "I'm a football fan and about that time I was watching my favorite team play. One of the officials threw a flag indicating a penalty—they were guilty of defensive holding! It was like a message from God saying, *'Don't be penalized for defensive holding!* Don't hold your daughter back. Let her become what she was meant to be!' So I let her go with my blessing!" he added.

Some of you are guilty of defensive holding. The person who listens to God and is open to His beautiful dreams is never penalized for defensive holding! Listen to Him and you will glisten!

> **God gives me the ability to listen and to choose the happy way, the right way, the way of joy!**

Exalt Courage

"How wonderful it is, how pleasant, when brothers live in harmony!"

Psalm 133:1

What is courage? We can all understand what courage is when we see a soldier fighting for our freedom as he heads for the front line. We can understand courage when we see a fire truck speeding down the street and the fireman climbing high on his ladder. We can understand courage when we see the police officer rushing through the black of the night to protect someone.

But there are other levels of courage. There is the courage to love, or the courage to forgive, or the courage of commitment.

What does courage mean to you? Create a special courage poem using the following format. The first line is one word—the title. Line two has two words which describe the title. Line three is three words and is an action phrase about the title. Line four has four words that describe your feelings about the title. Line five is one word that restates the title. Try it, using the word *Courage* as the title.

COURAGE

_____

_____ _____

_____ _____ _____

_____ _____ _____ _____

_____

> **I face today with courage—God's courage! I feel His power running through me!**

Exalt Courage

"Keep your eyes open for spiritual danger; stand true to the Lord; act like men; be strong."

1 Corinthians 16:13

There is not a city in America where you cannot pick up a telephone and dial for the correct time. In many cities you can even dial a number and receive the weather forecast. Along the coast, you can dial a number and find out the condition of the surf.

And no matter where you live in this country you can dial the area code 714, and the letters NEW HOPE anytime, day or night, and the phone will ring in the Tower of Hope on the Garden Grove Community Church campus. You can talk with a trained counselor in America's first 24 hour church telephone counseling program.

But did you know you could dial for courage? You don't have to remember any numbers, all you need to know is one letter—"C"! You can dial for courage when the doctor's report comes back and the cancer is malignant; or when your husband leaves you; or when you lose a precious child. You can! *Dial "C" for courage!* The "C" stands for Christ. All you need to do is turn to Him and courage will come to you from a source that transcends you.

God is listening. And He always gets our message. He gives us what we need. That's what Jesus Christ can do for you! Dial "C" for courage today!

> **God has given me a courageous, all-conquering spirit. He has given me the spirit of Jesus Christ. I am confident!**

Exalt Courage

"The godly are bold as lions!"

Proverbs 28:1

The judge was campaigning for reelection and was running on his record of integrity. He was a distinguished and honorable gentleman of no small charity. And his opponent was conducting a vicious, mud-smearing, unfair campaign against him.

At a news conference, a reporter stood and asked the judge, "Your Honor, do you know what your opponent is saying about you? Are you aware of the criticism he is leveling at you? Would you care to comment?"

The judge looked at his campaign counselors and the chairman of his committee. Then he looked at his audience and calmly replied: "Well, when I was a boy I had a dog. And every time the moon was full, that old hound dog would howl and bark at the things he saw in the bright face of the moon. We never did sleep very well those nights. He would bark and howl at the moon all night long." With that he concluded his remarks.

"That's beside the point," his campaign chairman impatiently said. "You haven't answered your critics!" The judge explained, "I just did! When the dog barked at the moon, *the moon kept right on shining!* I don't intend to say anything back to my critic. I'm going to keep right on shining—quietly and calmly, like the moon!"

That takes courage! That's the courage required to sail to the top and not worry about what people will say if you succeed or if you fail. Only God can give you that kind of courage!

I'm shining Lord. I can feel your courage within me.

Exalt Courage

*"We need have no fear of someone who loves us perfectly;
his perfect love for us eliminates all dread."*

1 John 4:18

It is often the fear of the unknown that saps the reservoir
of courage in many of us, even though we may strongly
desire to succeed. W. Clement Stone points out that it
takes time to succeed and it takes time to fail, but it takes
less time to succeed at something, even when we are afraid.
The secret of success is getting started.

When your courage starts to fade as you face some difficult task or situation, repeat *Do it Now!* to yourself over
and over again. Develop the habit of saying *Do it Now!*

Let's *Do it Now!* Finish each of the lines below and then
read what you have written, along with the words *Do it
Now!*

WHEN FACED WITH _____

I WILL DO IT NOW!

WHEN MY COURAGE FADES BECAUSE _____

_____

I WILL DO _____ NOW!

WHEN UNCERTAINTY HITS ME BECAUSE _____

_____

I WILL DO _____ NOW!

DO IT NOW!

Exàlt Courage

"God loves you very much . . . don't be afraid! Calm your-
self; be strong—yes, be strong!"

Daniel 10:19

"Here I am!" the young voice called out to the stranger
walking by. The little girl was barely two years old, lying
in bed hugging her teddy bear. Both of her tiny legs were
hanging in the air, in traction.

"Well, hello!" the new friend enthused. "I have brittle
bones," the tiny girl responded quickly. "This one is
broken. Last time it was that one," she said as she pointed
to her right leg. "I've had 22 fractures!"

By the time she was six, Charlotte had been in and out of
the hospital 85 times. She has a rare disease which means
her bones break very easily. By the time she was ten she
had over 200 fractures.

"I only saw her cry twice," a close friend of the family
said. Once when she had to miss her sister's wedding
because she fractured her arm. The other time was when
she made a community appeal to urge people to give so
crippled children could walk."

Charlotte never weighs more than fifty pounds, but she
pushed through high school, chose a university with ramps
for wheelchairs and graduated four years later Cum Laude!
She went on to law school and passed the state bar exam!
All fifty pounds of her. She has courage! She's so much in
love with life that she'll fight every day! Courage is the
back side of the coin of love!

**Courage fills my mind and heart, for I
know that God is my strength!**

Exalt Courage

"Don't be troubled or afraid."

John 14:27

Why do we exalt courage? Because every person who chooses to be brave inspires the rest of the human race! The entire human family is exalted, honored and dignified when someone fights a brave battle.

Lillian Dickson and her husband felt called by God to the island called Formosa. When they arrived, they talked to a government official in Social Services. He looked at this young and naive couple and laughed, "Look, go back to America. You can't possibly succeed here. There is no way!"

He stood up and walked over to the window and pointed outside. "Look, you can see the ocean. Helping people here in Formosa is like trying to change the ocean one bucket at a time!"

Young Lillian Dickson got out of her chair and said, "Well, then I am going to fill my bucket!" And they left the room. Fifty plus years later, her husband dead, Lillian is still filling her bucket. She has established over one thousand churches, schools and hospitals. It all happened because she and her husband had the courage and the willingness to fail!

If they had turned around and gone home, no one would have blamed them. But they stayed and faced possible futility. And Formosa is a better place today because of their courage!

Today I live courageously speaking only words of hope that will encourage others to more courage!

Exalt Courage

Turn, O Lord, my fears around.
Let them become a positive force
for good in my life until I—

Fear not that I might fail
　But fear rather that I might never dare
　to discover my potential.

Fear not that I might be hurt.
　But fear rather that I might never
　experience growing pains.

Fear not that I might live and lose.
　But fear rather that I might
　never love at all.

Fear not that people may laugh at my mistakes.
　But fear rather that God will say to me
　"O ye of little faith."

Fear not that I might fail if I try again.
　But fear rather that I might miss
　my greatest chance for happiness
　if I failed to give hope another opportunity.

Amen.

Scars Become Stars

"From being weaklings they become strong."
                       Hebrews 11:34 Phillips

A guide said to me one time some years ago in the Netherlands, "See that huge concrete plug in the dike? We had a leak there one time and the sea rushed in. Many people perished in the floods. But we plugged it with concrete—steel-reinforced concrete—and it'll never break there again."

A doctor said to me one time as he pointed to a nurse walking down the hall, "She's the best nurse we have. She works so hard and is so dedicated to the patients." Then, almost as an afterthought, he added, "I guess it has something to do with the fact that when she was a teenager she spent ten months on her back in this hospital."

Before my secretary, Lois Wendell, died of cancer, people would often tell me how much she had helped them as they faced the uncertainties of an operation. *Where she was weak, there she became strong!*

You can turn your scars into stars. Your hurts can become halos. The principle here is that if you want to live an emotionally healthy and happy life you must discover how to handle the hurts that come. The writer of the Hebrews assures us that our weaknesses can be turned into strength!

**I am one with unlimited strength.
God helps me turn my scars into stars!**

Scars Become Stars

"For when I am weak, then I am strong—the less I have, the more I depend on him."

2 Corinthians 12:10

There are several types of weaknesses. Some relate to hurts caused by other people. Some are simply caused by life and its natural processes. Then there are weaknesses that relate to qualities in our personality. Perhaps we are very trusting, or our feelings are very sensitive. And because of these qualities, we find we are easily hurt.

What are some of the weaknesses in your life? Have you ever considered the potential strengths represented by these qualities? Let's list some of them and then think of all the possible strengths that could be associated with those "weaknesses."

MY WEAKNESS	POTENTIAL STRENGTH

I can feel my attitude changing.
I am turning my former weakness into a
strength. My scars are becoming stars!

Scars Become Stars

"The weakness of God is stronger than men."
                              1 Corinthians 1:25 KJV

Here are some sound principles that will help you turn your scars into stars. First, don't curse life's hurts! I hear it so often: "He's been going downhill ever since his son died." Or, "She's been drinking a lot since her husband left her." Or, "He dropped out of high school when he was a senior because he didn't make the football team."

There are many ways to curse our hurts, but when you curse them you become bitter. Hurts can either make us bitter or better—don't curse your hurts!

Second, don't rehearse and nurse your hurts. A lady called my office and asked to see me. Her husband had died two years before and she had been crying inside for two long, painful years. She said, "Dr. Schuller, I know you are so busy. I just didn't want to bother you." I put my arm around her as I led her into my office.

As she talked, she related everything that had happened up to the time of her husband's death—everything! She knew every detail. Finally she opened her purse and took out a sheet of paper and read to me the words of her doctor as he had explained to her the cause of her husband's death. I cried with her!

We had prayed, and then I said, "I want you to do something. I want you to tear up that piece of paper and throw it away. It's time you stopped *rehearsing* and *nursing* your hurt!" Weeks later when I saw her again, she smiled and whispered, "Thanks, I feel better already!"

**Lord, the past is past!
Thank you for the newness of today!**

Scars Become Stars

"Share each other's troubles and problems, and so obey our Lord's command."

Galatians 6:2

You probably can't help it when the hurt comes, but you can help it if the hurt lasts. Through the power of God and through the power of prayer you can handle any hurt!

A friend of mine was having a problem with a business competitor. All kinds of negative emotions were coming in. I suggested to him that he pray about it.

"And what do I pray?" he asked me, "that my competitor will succeed?" I knew that didn't sound right, so I suggested, "I don't know, *just pray that God will tell you what to pray.* Ask God what you should pray."

Several days later, he said, "I woke up last night at 2:00 a.m. and I knew how to pray!" "What was it?" I asked. "God gave me the prayer—here it is: 'Dear God, make that person into exactly the person you want him to be and cause his business to develop just the way you would like to see it develop!' " He went on, "That completely cured me. If that guy's business succeeds, I can't be angry about it because I prayed that God's plan would be worked out."

Now, if you have a hurt, and if you have prayed about it and your praying hasn't helped, then you have prayed the wrong prayer. Start now and ask God what you ought to pray. He'll help you *disburse* your hurts by placing them in His care!

> **My hurts are fading as I turn them over to God—one-by-one!**

Scars Become Stars

"Behold, I have given you authority . . . and nothing shall hurt you!"

Luke 10:19 RSV

What are some of the hurts you are still carrying? Take the time to write a description below: _____

_____

_____

_____

_____

_____

_____

_____

_____

Now, look back over what you have written. Stop and commit through prayer, each hurt to the healing power of God. Then in big bold letters, write "CANCELED" across what you have written!

> I am a child of God.
> Nothing can hurt me for
> He takes care of His children!

Scars Become Stars

"We, too, are weak in our bodies, as he was, but now we live and are strong, as he is, and have all of God's power to use."

2 Corinthians 13:4

The other day I was watching as the elevator doors opened. I had just stepped out of my office in time to see a young mother with a little girl pulling at her skirt. The mother looked busy . . . she seemed to be rushed, and even a little harassed.

I asked my secretary, "Who is she? What is she doing here at this time of day?" My secretary reminded me that she was in charge of our Helping Hand project.

This young mother spends hours at the church collecting tin cans full of soup and vegetables. People call in to our 24-hour counseling service and say they have nothing—no food. We have a policy that we will not give people money, but we will give them food and groceries. This young mother manages this whole operation.

My secretary reminded me, "You remember she wrote you a letter some months ago that really moved you. She thanked God for our wonderful congregation." I remembered. Her husband had been flat on his back for months, unable to work. She had a baby who became sick and she couldn't work either. The church heard about her and the ladies brought breakfast, lunch and dinner for them, day after day, week after week.

She found a way to repay their love! And time after time, when I look at a great person, I say, *somewhere that person was hurt, and turned that hurt into a halo!*

I belong to God. All that happens to me is part of His plan for my good. I feel His strength flowing within!

Scars Become Stars

"Clothe yourself with strength from God."

Isaiah 52:1

Some people *curse* their hurts, *rehearse* and *nurse* them, or *disburse* them by sending them on their way. The best way to turn a hurt into a halo, a scar into a star, is to turn it over to God and allow Him to turn it inside out. He will *reverse* it so that it becomes a star in your crown!

Write a prayer today that expresses your feelings as you turn over to God any and all of your hurts.

Dear God, _____

_____

_____

_____

_____

_____

_____

_____

_____

_____

_____

> **I give my hurts to God
> and He turns them into strength!**

Know Where You're Going

"For God is at work within you, helping you want to obey him, and then helping you do what he wants."

Philippians 2:13

The man who booted the longest field goal in the history of pro football wasn't supposed to be able to do it. But no one told him that, and he did the impossible.

Tom Dempsey was born with only half a right foot and with a deformed right arm and hand. And even though he successfully overcame his handicap and played football in high school and in college, he was turned down by the professional teams. They looked at his right side and said, "You are not professional material."

But he refused to accept their word. He says, "I have learned never to give up. So many times in life in sports, I have seen things turn around because someone persevered and has kept faith. My parents taught me that kind of faith.

In 1970, in a game between the Detroit Lions and the New Orleans Saints, the Saints were about to upset the Lions. With only 11 seconds left, Detroit took the lead by one point. It looked like the game was over. The Saints had 2 seconds left and were on their own 45 yard line. In came Tom Dempsey to kick a field goal.

Up to that time the longest field goal had been 56 yards. This one would be 63 yards. The goal posts were so far away that Tom didn't even know he had made it until the official raised his arms. The Saints won because no one told Tom it was impossible!

**God's will is surging within me.
I want to please Him!**

Know Where You're Going

*"Beloved, we are God's children now; it does not yet
appear what we shall be."*

1 John 3:2 RSV

Possibility thinkers begin setting goals by examining
realistically their God-given talents. A story is told about a
farmer who, while trying to decide on his future, saw a
cloud formation in the sky which formed the letters "P"
and "C". He interpreted this sign to mean "Preach Christ."

He became a preacher, but because he lacked the
God-given talents and the necessary spiritual gifts, he
failed. He concluded that the letters must have stood for
"Plow Corn." So he returned to his great work of feeding
a nation.

On the other side of the coin, a friend of our family is
over 60 years old. Two years ago she started taking piano
lessons. Today, she's good enough to be giving beginning
piano lessons to little children. Because she has such a
sweet, pleasant spirit, the children love her. She is
a success!

These two stories illustrate some very important principles for goal-setting:

1. Discover the undiscovered talents within you. They
are there! Look for them.

2. Don't underestimate your talent. It takes all kinds of
abilities to keep God's world moving.

3. Dedicate your talent to God. He can do a lot with a
little if it's turned over to Him!

4. Start today!

**I am an important part of
God's plans for today!**

Know Where You're Going

*"God has given each of us the ability to do certain
things well."*

Romans 12:6

Saint Paul urges each of us to make an honest evalua-
tion of ourselves. A helpful bit of advice in setting goals is
to begin where you are. You find out where you are by
checking out the talents and abilities God has given you.
With that information in hand, you are ready to plan
where you're going.

You can begin by listing some of the things you enjoy
doing. Then write down the abilities you have that help
you enjoy doing these things.

THINGS I ENJOY DOING	ABILITIES I HAVE

**I am glad for all that God is
planning for me!**

Know Where You're Going

*"Be strong! Be courageous! Do not be afraid of them! For
the Lord your God will be with you. He will neither fail
you nor forsake you."*

Deuteronomy 31:6

Along with your talents, you need to consider your
challenges. The challenges God sends your way often
appear, at the outset, as problems, troubles, or difficulties. Only as you exercise possibility thinking will you
begin to discover the universal principle that every problem is an opportunity! Thus difficulties become challenges
to do something constructive, or to become a bigger,
broader, better person than ever before.

As you consider setting personal goals, consider the
challenging spot you're in. If you are in the hospital, your
goal today may be to raise an arm, tomorrow you'll try to
raise a leg. Then your goal will be to roll over on your side,
then getting up and going to the bathroom yourself.
Finally, you will have as your goal walking in the hallway—on your way home!

INCH BY INCH, ANYTHING'S A CINCH!

The important thing is your attitude toward the spot
you're in right now. If you think "it's impossible," then
your problem is really a problem! Bu if you "think
possibilities," then your problem is really an opportunity
for you to triumph! And triumph is made up of two
words: TRY and UMPH.

> If I never know personal problems,
> I'll never be able to know the joy of
> personal triumph! Today with God's
> help, I will triumph!

Know Where You're Going

"If then you have been raised with Christ, seek the things that are above, where Christ is."

Colossians 3:1 RSV

So far, you've considered your talents and your challenges. Before setting personal goals, you also need to consider your values.

A young lady had just finished her college education and started working. During the first months, she spent every cent she earned on clothes. Her father urged her to put some of her money in a savings account, arguing that thrift was a virtue.

She insisted that clothes made the woman and therefore she had to have a beautiful wardrobe. The argument reached a stalemate. Finally, the desperate girl turned to her brother and asked, "What should I do—put the money in the bank or buy clothes?"

His immediate reply was, "Put your money wherever it will draw the most interest!"

Each individual—the father, the young woman, and her brother—expressed their sense of values in their discussion. The father valued thrift. The daughter valued appearances. The brother valued his neck—he didn't want to get caught between his father and his sister.

Sometimes our values are inconsistent, like the man who had just been caught in a daring burglary. The officer asked him why he had tried such a complicated crime alone.

"Well," replied the prisoner, "where can you find a man who's honest enough to trust for a job like this?"

I enter this day with my sights set high!

Know Where You're Going

"Let heaven fill your thoughts; don't spend your time worrying about things down here."

Colossians 3:2

What do you value? If you were faced with a choice, what would you keep and what would you let go of? Suppose you are suddenly faced with a fire in your home. You only have time to rescue eight items. What would they be? Write down the first things that come to mind:

1. _____

2. _____

3. _____

4. _____

5. _____

6. _____

7. _____

8. _____

Now go back through your list and think about each one. How would you rank each item? Which would be first? Which one was eight on your list? As you think about each item, what does each one say about *your* values? What value system are you living by?

**My values are in tune with God's values!
I am doing my part to live as God's child
in this world!**

Know Where You're Going

"The Kingdom of God is within you."

Luke 17:21

Deep within you lies the power of God. And God waits to give you what you need to make your dreams come true.

BELIEVE IN A BIG GOD! Then make your goals and plans big enough for God to fit into them. Simply ask yourself and God, what would be a great thing for me to do with the rest of my life? Do it now and write down your answer:

_____

_____

_____

_____

_____

_____

Decide now to do it. If you need more education, get it. If it's money you need, find it! If it's talent you need, learn the skills or find someone to share your dream with that has the skills. The important thing is to begin—today!

> **God gives me dominion over
> every limitation!**

Grow Faith

"For we walk by faith, not by sight."

2 Corinthians 5:7 RSV

I have had many people say to me, "Dr. Schuller, you talk about possibility thinking, and you say that faith moves mountains. Yet I cry and bleed because my mountain has not moved. Was Jesus wrong? Did He make a mistake?"

My immediate reply is, "We all have a lot to learn, especially when it comes to faith and possibility thinking. For when Jesus says, 'You can say to this mountain, "Move" and it would go far away! Nothing is impossible with God!' "

Now one of the first things we need to learn is that faith has five phases. And these five phases are all part of the process. We often quit in the middle of the process, but faith never quits on us. We may fail faith, but faith never fails. However, if you cut out one phase and don't stay with it through all five phases, you will be disappointed with the results.

Faith is like a seed. If a seed is not planted, it won't bear fruit. You must first plant the seed—that's the first phase. Unless the seed is watered it won't sprout. That's the second phase. The growth begins, but it must be nourished—phase three. The fourth phase involves the proper climate to make certain the buds form. And when all phases are tended to properly, you reach phase five—the harvest!

Now when we talk about the five phases of faith, we'll use different words to describe each phase—that's our project in the days that follow.

I am patient. When my faith seems weak, I keep trusting and believing for I know that with God all things are possible!

Grow Faith

"He who trusts in me shall possess the land and inherit my Holy Mountain."

Isaiah 57:13

The first phase of faith is the *nesting* phase. An egg is dropped, an idea is born, a thought comes into the nest of the mind.

Now for some people that is the only phase of faith they ever experience. The egg is never hatched! Their faith never goes beyond the nesting phase for these people simply will not do anything about the potential possibility seeking to be born. The idea comes and they let it go. It dies in the nest!

What idea is nesting in your mind today? What beautiful possibility is God seeking to bring to your attention. Stop and meditate awhile and then write down the idea God is placing in the nest of your mind.

_____

_____

_____

_____

_____

_____

Remember, the nesting phase is only the beginning!

> My mind is alive with ideas
> and dreams. God is opening up
> new vistas before me!

Grow Faith

*"Blessed is the man who trusts in the Lord and has made
the Lord his hope and confidence. He is like a tree planted
along a riverbank, with its roots reaching deep into the
water."*

Jeremiah 17:7, 8

The second phase of faith is the *testing* phase. This is the
time to ask questions. And your questions will arise out of
your value system. I have lectured on this to students and
leaders in schools and industry. And I always emphasize
that decision-making is easy if your value system is clear
and unclouded.

When you know the right question, you can know
immediately if you have a good idea or a bad idea. Here
are the three questions I use. Ask them of yourself and
your idea.

1. Is it really necessary? _____

_____

2. Is it needed? _____

_____

3. Is it a beautiful idea? _____

_____

If you are satisfied with your answers, then your idea
has passed through the second phase—the testing of faith!

My faith is growing! I am more confident
as I test my idea against important
questions and know that God is
guiding me!

Grow Faith

"The apostles said to the Lord, 'We need more faith; tell us how to get it.' "

Luke 17:5

The third phase of faith is the *investing* phase. Now is the time to make a commitment and move forward! You will need to commit time, money, energy—and possibly your most valuable item, your prestige, to the project.

When you have to put up risk capital, you suddenly run short of faith. It is easy to dream dreams and test them for their value. But when you have to invest time, money, energy and prestige, faith can easily begin to falter. When it does, remember that faith will not fail you, but you will fail the test of your faith when you back away from making your investment.

It's easy to get cold feet when you have to risk something. But if your faith is going to grow, you must successfully pass through the *investing* phase of faith.

What will your idea cost? Make as accurate a list as possible.

_____   _____

_____   _____

_____   _____

_____   _____

_____   _____

I can feel courage within me undergirding my faith as I willingly make the commitment to invest!

Grow Faith

"Those who trust in the Lord are steady as Mount Zion, unmoved by any circumstance."

Psalm 125:1

Watch out for the fourth phase—the *arresting* phase of faith. Suddenly problems surround you, troubles block you, defeat seems almost certain as you begin to think you have bitten off more than you can chew. This is when you wonder if you've made a mistake with your investment.

The arresting phase of faith is God's way of testing us before the final harvest. Will we really be grateful? Will we be humble? Can He trust us with success?

My personal testimony is that every idea that ever came from God in my short life took a lot of faith for me to be willing to invest my time, energy and reputation. And everytime I made the commitment to invest, I inevitably ran into a problem where the whole momentum of the project was arrested just when success seemed around the corner. I was suddenly stopped in my tracks. It looked like I would sink!

In this fourth phase of faith God is testing our *reliability* and our *humility*. So be patient when trouble comes and be thankful God is at work.

I do not believe that God will ever give you an idea that will not run into the arresting phase of faith. But remember, *God's delays are not God's denials!* Hang on! Stay with it! Keep on believing!

> Forgive me Lord, for my doubts. Already I can feel confidence within me as I recognize You are working in my life!

Grow Faith

Don't Quit

"When things go wrong as they sometimes will,
When the road you're trudging seems all uphill,
When the funds are low and the debts are high,
And you want to smile, but you have to sigh,
When cares are pressing you down a bit,
Rest if you must, but don't you quit!

Life is strange with its twists and turns,
As everyone of us sometimes learns.
And many a failure turns about,
When he might have won if he stuck it out.
Don't give up though the pace seems slow,
You may succeed with another blow.

Success is failure turned inside out,
The silver tint of the clouds of doubt.
And you never can tell how close you are,
It may be near when it seems so far.
So stick to the fight when you're hardest hit,
It's when things get worse that you must not quit!"

Grow Faith

*"So I pray for you . . . that God who gives you hope will
keep you happy and full of peace as you believe in him!"*
                                                    Romans 15:13

The final stage of faith is the *cresting* phase. The crest
comes when we reach the mountaintop and achieve
success. All the problems are solved. Salvation comes. The
habit is broken. The money is here! The project is accomplished! The chains are broken and deliverance has come.

Look how these five phases of faith worked in Christ's
life. His idea of His ministry started to come together when
He was 12 years old. He knew that God wanted Him to do
something. The *nesting* phase occurred when He realized
He must be about His Father's business.

The *testing* phase came when He spent 40 days in the
wilderness being tempted by Satan. The investing time
came as He spent several years stalking the plains and
deserts, preaching, teaching and touching lives. He
experienced great popularity with the crowds.

But then came the *arresting* phase as people turned away
from Him. The agony in the Garden at Gethsemane and
the tremendous shame of the cross led to Jesus crying out,
"My God, why have you forsaken me?" It looked like His
dream was finished.

But then came the *cresting* phase. He arose on the third
day! Easter morning was the crest! And He is alive today!
Be patient. God is at work. As you keep on believing, you
will reach the crest!

> Almost there, Lord. I can see the top!
> I can feel Your spirit driving me onward
> and upward. Thank you!

Power Steering Living

"Let this mind be in you, which was also in Christ Jesus."
Philippians 2:5 KJV

I can remember the first time I drove a car with power steering. Suddenly, maneuvering the difficult corners was simple, and managing my way through heavy traffic was no problem. Turning the wheels and settling the course became easy, calm and controlled.

There are some people today that seem to live their lives just like that. They can make decisions swiftly, and maneuver their way through the traffic of frustration and problems with calmness and control. With smooth power they move ahead toward their easily determined goals and objectives. I call this *Power Steering Living*.

Then there are others, frustrated and insecure, without Power Steering Living. They simply cannot turn their life in any direction. Maneuvering through the traffic of frustration and problems is tiresome and laborious.

Why do some people have power steering while others don't? Here's the answer: *Power Steering people have achieved mind clearing!* Mind clearing produces power steering. When your mind is clear, you will have the power to steer your life without any difficulty!

I quiet myself and feel all fear and tension leaving me. My mind is clear and available for God's power!

Power Steering Living

"My meditation of him shall be sweet: I will be glad in the Lord."

Psalm 104:34 KJV

Look up the following verses and write down what they say to you about meditation and praying:

Psalm 1:2

Psalm 4:4

Psalm 19:14

Psalm 49:3

Psalm 119:11, 15, 16

Psalm 139:17

Psalm 143:5

I fill my mind with thoughts of Thee,
O Lord, and I am filled with joy!

Power Steering Living

"I recall the many miracles he did for me so long ago.
Those wonderful deeds are constantly in my thoughts. I
cannot stop thinking about them."

Psalm 77:11, 12

How do you maintain the process of mind clearing? Let me answer that question this way: All fuel needs to be filtered before it can produce power. There can be no power without fuel. Whether it's gas to an engine or thoughts that come as energy to the brain; all power-producing organisms require fuel! And all fuel needs to be filtered or the power-potential will diminish.

A good friend of mine invented and patented a Vacco filter. So the fuel in all the space vehicles that carried men to the moon was cleansed through this filter. And the fuel in all the nuclear submarines, cruise missiles, nuclear generating plants, and satellites goes through his remarkable filter. It's the only filter used!

What makes this filter different! For one thing, it operates on the horizontal. And as the air and the fuel pass through, this filter traps particles as small as 1/25th of a micron. (It takes 25 microns to make a thousandth of an inch.) It can literally filter out bacteria. There's no other filter like it!

But there is something that is even greater than the Vacco filter. It can screen out something even smaller than bacteria. It can even eliminate negative thoughts. It's Jesus Christ. He wants to come into your mind and filter out all the negative thoughts and influences that would take away your power!

> **Jesus Christ is cleansing my thoughts**
> **of all negative forces. Power is being**
> **restored to full capacity!**

Power Steering Living

*"Fix your thoughts on what is true and good and right.
Think about things that are pure and lovely, and dwell on
the fine, good things in others."*

Philippians 4:8

Saint Paul is very direct. He tells the people in Philippi
exactly what they are to think about. His advice is still
right on target!

Imagine that a friend of yours has come to you to share a
problem with his or her thought life. Using the verse at the
top of the page, write down what you would say to them:

_____

_____

_____

_____

_____

_____

_____

_____

Think a bit now about how your advice could be applied
to your own thought life. Remember, Power Steering
Living comes from mind clearing!

> **Evil, negative thoughts are fading.
> Pure, clean, positive thoughts are
> growing stronger!**

Power Steering Living

"Think about all you can praise God for and be glad about."

Philippians 4 : 8

One of the best ways to clear your mind for Power Steering Living is to concentrate on all the good things you can praise God for in your life and in the lives of those around you. Today is PRAISE DAY! Make a list of everything you can praise God for and be glad about!

I PRAISE GOD FOR

_____

_____

_____

_____

_____

_____

_____

_____

_____

_____

_____

My whole body, soul and spirit praise God!

Power Steering Living

*"Every morning tell him, 'Thank you for your kindness,'
and every evening rejoice in all his faithfulness."*

Psalm 92:2

E. Stanley Jones tells in his book, *Abundant Living*, this principle: "I am spiritually relaxed because I believe the central hypothesis of my life is right. Life is one long verification of that central hypothesis. This fact gives an inner sense of steadiness.

"This attitude toward life was tested in an airplane over St. Louis when we circled above the clouds for two hours, trying to land. The ceiling was so low that we could not get under. I had time to think. So I wrote down a life conclusion: 'I am up in this plane and we have been circling over these clouds for about two hours. If we do not land safely I would like to leave my last will and testament to my friends and fellow followers of Christ. There is peace, perfect peace. Apart from my unfaithfulness to the highest, there are no regrets about the general course of my life.

" 'Life with Christ is the way to live. In this hour there is assurance—there is God underneath all the uncertainties of human existence. So I rest in God. God's best to you all. Living or dying I am His—His alone. Glory! Signed, E. Stanley Jones.'

"I meet today, today. I do not telescope all next week into today. Someone said, 'The load of Tomorrow, added to that of Yesterday, carried Today, makes the strongest falter.' "

E. Stanley Jones knew how to clear his mind for Power Steering Living!

> **Today, I will live today.
> The past gives me courage, the future is
> in God's hand!**

Power Steering Living

*"I lie awake at night thinking of you—of how much you
have helped me—and how I rejoice through the night
beneath the protecting shadow of your wings."*
                                        Psalm 63:6, 7

I read recently the documented story of a man who
accidentally trapped himself inside a refrigerated railroad
car. He became frantic, pounding on the door and scream-
ing, but nobody heard him.

He knew that no human being could survive in that kind
of an environment so he settled into a corner of the car and
began to scrawl his last thoughts on the wall.

"I am becoming very cold. I do not have long to live
anymore. I can tell that death is coming close to me. I can
feel it very near. These may well be my last words." And
they were!

When the refrigerator car door was opened, they found
the man dead. But here's what's so amazing. The refriger-
ation unit had not been working for a month. There was
still enough oxygen in the railroad car to sustain life, even
when they found his body. But the most amazing thing was
that the lowest temperature during the man's entrapment
was 58 degrees! He did not die of cold. He did not die of
suffocation. Only one thing killed him. FEAR!! That fear,
along with the illusion that he was freezing inside the railroad car!

Psychologists are beginning to pay attention to this
phenomena. Centuries ago, God revealed to us that "As a
man thinks in his heart, so is he!" Clear your mind for
Power Steering Living!

> My thoughts dwell on the realization of
> God as the source of my every need.

Change!

"Great is your faith! Be it done for you as you desire."
Matthew 15:28 RSV

Istanbul, once called Constantinople, is a beautiful city. Over the centuries, it has always been one of the great cities of the world. When you enter the harbor by ship, as I did some years ago, it is an inspiring sight to see. You enter the Golden Horn and sail up the Sea of Marmara. From there you can catch the view of the sun reflected off the gold domes of the mosques that were originally built as great cathedrals. Many of them were built over 700 years ago and still stand today as glorious monuments to the people and their faith.

There was a time in the ancient days when insecure rulers of Constantinople wanted to make sure that they could keep the enemy out. They performed a remarkable feat. They created the largest and heaviest chain ever built by human beings. The links are about a foot and a half long and about two inches thick. This monstrous chain was built by hand and then draped across the harbor to keep foreign ships out of their territory. People still marvel at how they were able to maneuver something so bulky and heavy.

As I listened to the story of that chain, I could see people drawing chains across the harbor of their mind. These chains keep out new thoughts and ideas. They keep them from being open to change. If you are bound by chains, you can break them and change!

> **My heart is open to all the wonderful possibilities of change!**

Change!

"Sing unto him a new song . . . for our heart shall rejoice in him."

Psalm 33:3, 21 KJV

Picture your mind as a harbor. There is a channel leading in and there is a harbormaster keeping close watch on everything that comes and goes. Draw a picture of what the "harbor of your mind" looks like. What wreckage of the past threatens to block the channel? When do you draw the chains across the opening? Symbolize these things in a picture, or simply list them in the space below.

Lord, I have fired the harbormaster. You are now in control!

Change!

"Yes, you must be a new and different person, holy and good. Clothe yourself with this new nature."

Ephesians 4:24

One of the greatest men in Judea today is a Palestinian who was educated at Cambridge University and then returned to Jerusalem to establish his own business.

Musa Alami did quite well by his own standards until the political upheaval. He had to vacate Jerusalem and live in a refugee camp along with a lot of other poor Palestine refugees. But rather than take that kind of a static, non-productive lifestyle, he decided to be a possibility thinker.

He stood on top of a mountain and gazed on the hills of Moab. He saw only one trickle of blue water flowing in the vast wasteland—the Jordan River flowing from Galilee to the Dead Sea.

With all that desert, Musa thought, "If only there was more water." Then he came up with an incredible and impossible idea. "Why not dig for sub-surface water, like they did in California?" So he talked some of his more daring friends to go out into the desert and start digging.

"You fools," people mocked. "There is no water in Jordan!" But Musa and his companions kept on digging. After months, they found a place where the sand felt cool and seemed to change color. Could it be water? One more shovelful and the water began to seep in, covering the dry soil. Today Musa farms in the desert—all because he removed the chains from his mind and sought change!

I relax and let the life-changing power of God flow through me!

Change!

"When God the Father, with glorious power, brought him back to life again, you were given his wonderful new life to enjoy."

Romans 6:4

Inventory time! Let's do a checkup on how much we have changed already. Recognizing that we never reach perfection, fill in your own testimony of the changes God has already brought about in your life.

BEFORE I MET CHRIST, I WAS	TODAY, I AM BECOMING MORE

My spirits soar as I see what great things God is doing in my life!

Change!

"Now you can really serve God; not in the old way, mechanically obeying a set of rules, but in the new way, with all your hearts and minds."

Romans 7:6

I have met many people all over the world who can put on a good show, but until they change their thinking, they aren't going any place. They may have lots of style, but their thinking is what really makes the difference. And their minds are chained.

Some people hang on to their chains. They allow themselves to remain bound. I was born into a poor family. We had no electricity—we couldn't afford it. We used kerosene lamps!

I don't remember getting gifts at Christmastime. We went to church and I got some candy in Sunday School. At home we made a few things for each other, but Christmas wasn't a time for piles of presents. We knew what poverty was!

But I can say to you today that the past does not bind the present! You can change! Whether you inherit poverty, oppression, prejudice, physical limitations, or whatever, you don't have to stay locked up and bound by these chains!

I'll tell you why. Because you are a child of God! And He can break the chains that keep you from changing where you really want to experience change. Ask Him right now to help you.

I let go and let God take over in my life. The freshness of His presence fills me with anticipation for today!

Change!

People
who never change their minds
are either perfect to begin with
or stubborn forever after.

So I'm willing, wanting, and waiting
to change into the person
you want me to be, Lord.

Amen

Change!

"It does not yet appear what we shall be, but we know that when he appears we shall be like him, for we shall see him as he is."

1 John 3:2 RSV

Do you know where Arabian horses come from? They are such spectacular, gorgeous creatures. Legend says that the prophet Mohammed decided that he wanted to breed the finest horses on the planet earth, so he searched the world over for one hundred striking mares.

After he collected these beautiful animals, he led them to the top of a mountain where he corralled them. Directly below them was a cool stream which they could only see and smell. He deprived them of water until they were wild with thirst. Then, and only then, did he lift the gate allowing all one hundred beasts to take off madly for the water.

All you could see were thundering, stampeding horses with tails flying in the wind, necks arched, nostrils flaring and mouths foaming, pulling themselves through clouds of spraying dust.

Just before the stampeding herd reached the water, Mohammed put a bugle to his lips and blew with all his might. All of the horses kept on running except for four mares who dug their hoofs into the ground and stopped. With mouths foaming and necks trembling, they froze, waiting for the next command. "These four mares will be the seeds of a new breed, and I will call them Arabian!" Mohammed cried out!

A common person becomes uncommon simply because he hears a different bugle call! Listen to Christ's bugle and He will call you to greatness!

> **My chains are broken
> and the changes are beautiful!**

Gratitude

"I will bless the Lord and not forget the glorious things he does for me."

Psalm 103:2

When I was a child, in the 30's, the drought swept into Iowa from the Dakotas. The winds became our enemy, peeling off the dry, rich, black soil and swirling it like drifting dunes into the gullies and canyons of our fields. We prayed for rain, but rain never came. We walked around our farm with white towels over our faces to keep from suffocating in the driving dust.

Then harvest season came. My father would normally harvest a hundred wagons-full of corn. But I remember the harvest that year. My father harvested a meager one-half wagon-load.

You know what happened? I'll never forget it. Seated at the dinner table with his calloused hands holding ours, my father looked up and thanked God. He said, "I thank you God that I have lost nothing. For I have regained the seed I planted in the springtime!" He planted a half wagon-load of seed; he harvested a half wagon-load in the fall!

While the other farmers were saying, "We lost 90 or 100 loads," my father told me, *"Never count up the might-have-beens* or you'll be defeated. Never look at what you have lost, look at what you have left!" The attitude of gratitude releases dynamic power in the person who is thankful.

I am looking at what I have and Lord, I am grateful for Your blessings.

Gratitude

"Oh, thank the Lord, for he's so good! His lovingkindness is forever!"

Psalm 118:1

How's your attitude of gratitude working today? Are you looking at what you have or at the might-have-beens? Let's practice! Start on this page, and then use extra paper when this page is full, and begin to list all the things you can think of that you have and for which you are grateful. Now add the names of persons you're grateful for! When you have finished, stop, and like the psalmist, say, "Thank the Lord, for he's so good!"

1. _____   9. _____

2. _____   10. _____

3. _____   11. _____

4. _____   12. _____

5. _____   13. _____

6. _____   14. _____

7. _____   15. _____

8. _____   16. _____

> Lord, I thought I had so little, but You have made me rich in ways I hadn't noticed before today. Thank you!

Gratitude

"Who but God can give me strength?"

Psalm 108:10

A friend of mine told me the story of a mother who came from Hawaii to visit the United States. She and her sons were traveling across the country by train. The little boy sat and talked with a distinguished gentleman, who later told her, "You've got a fine boy there. When he grows up, he ought to be a lawyer. He's smart. In fact, he ought to go to Stanford University. When he grows up, you just let me know if I can help."

The years passed. The young boy never forgot those words. When he graduated from high school, he wrote this man and reminded him of his promise. The man, Herbert Hoover, kept his promise. When Ike Sutton graduated, he wrote Herbert Hoover and asked him how he could express his gratitude. Hoover, a Republican, said, "Go back to Hawaii and enter politics. Run for office as a Republican and keep running until you win!"

Now, Hawaii has always voted heavily for Democrats. But Ike Sutton ran for office. He lost, but he kept running. Then came 1974 and he decided to run again and a miracle happened. He won!

His attitude of gratitude gave him *surviving* power. He survived eleven elections until he finally won. Gratitude gives you *surviving* power as well. Keep on keeping on until you win!

> I will not give up! I have too much to be
> thankful for to be a quitter!

Gratitude

"How precious it is, Lord, to realize that you are thinking about me constantly!"

Psalm 139:17

The attitude of gratitude releases the dynamic power that helps you survive. Gratitude also releases *reviving* power. You can find the power to start again when you feel like quitting. You can pick up the pieces and bounce back to make a come back.

When do you feel like quitting? Think about the situation a moment and then write dcown some of the pressures that cause you to feel like quitting:

_____

_____

Now, think about that discouraging situation and identify everything about that situation for which you can be thankful. This will be difficult, but practice the attitude of gratitude and write them down:

_____

_____

_____

I fill my mind with thoughts of gratitude concerning God, the people I know and the circumstances that surround me.

Gratitude

"I press on toward the goal for the prize of the upward call of God in Christ Jesus."

Philippians 3:14 RSV

The attitude of gratitude releases the dynamic power of surviving and reviving. Gratitude also gives you *striving* power. When you are revived through gratitude, suddenly you discover the energy to keep *striving*.

How do you strive? Saint Paul said he was pressing on toward a goal. Goals gave him striving power. He wanted to really know Jesus Christ (Philippians 3:10). He wanted to preach in Spain (Romans 15:24). He wanted his fellow Jews to believe Jesus Christ was the promised Messiah (Romans 9-11). Saint Paul had a number of goals.

What are your goals? Are you happy with your goals? If not, you're free to set new goals. Make your goals big enough for God to fit in! Ask God to help you describe two important goals for your life today. Then write them down:

1._____

_____

2._____

_____

Now strive onward and upward to meet your goals today—with God's help!

> My eyes are clear and bright as I look at the goals God and I have set.

Gratitude

"But thanks be to God, who gives us the victory through our Lord Jesus Christ."

1 Corinthians 15:57 RSV

I was home from college for the summer when a tornado dropped out of the sky like a slithering snake and wormed its way across our farm. We had enough warning to jump into the car and escape with our lives. But that black serpentine cloud dropped its poisonous head and sucked up all nine buildings on our farm, including our farmhouse.

When we drove back after the tornado was gone, we found only white foundations remaining, lying on a clean patch of black ground. Everything my father and mother had worked for was gone.

That night our family gathered. We held hands and prayed. My father prayed, "Oh, God, I thank you that not a life was lost! Not a human bone was broken. We have lost nothing that cannot be regained. And through the storm we have kept everything that would be irreplaceable—especially our faith!"

My father's attitude of gratitude gave him *driving* power. He went into town and bought an old house that was to be demolished. We took it apart board by board, nail by nail, and rebuilt it over the empty hole in the ground that was the basement of our previous house.

Driving power—the ability to make bold decisions and move forward confidently in the face of tremendous odds.

I awake to a new day filled with abundant driving power. I am confident.

Gratitude

"Whatever you wish will happen! And the light of heaven will shine upon the road ahead of you."

Job 22:28

The attitude of gratitude releases dynamic power! Gratitude releases *arriving* power. You make it!

And when you arrive, you will have also developed the great qualities of character—humility and unselfishness. Humility because you realize you did not arrive through your efforts alone. It took team work. Unselfishness because gratitude is nothing more than saying, "I didn't really do it. Thank you for your help!" Gratitude is saying thank you to this person, to your friends, to your community and country, and to God.

It is impossible to become a vain, egotistical, selfish person if you maintain an attitude of gratitude! To whom are you grateful?

I am grateful to: _____

_____

_____

I will let them know by: _____

_____

The light of God illuminates my mind. I see people who have helped me and I am filled with gratitude.

Welcome The Unexpected

"Whatever you do or say, let it be as a representative of the Lord Jesus."

Colossians 3 : 17

I recall a woman who had recently lost her husband. They had been married for many years and had planned to retire and travel together. They had all their plans made and were looking forward to finally realizing a lifelong dream coming true. But a month after he retired, the husband suddenly died.

All of life seemed to come to an end for the wife. She put a tombstone on her husband's grave inscribed with the words, "The light of my life has gone out." I am sure many of you know the feelings she experienced.

But with the passage of time and the wise counsel of friends, this woman came alive again. The unexpected and unwelcome interruption lost its sting. Two years later her pastor married her to another wonderful man and watched them as they enthusiastically anticipated building a new life.

"Pastor," she said, "I'm going to have to change that line on the tombstone."

"No," replied her pastor, "I think all you have to do is add one other line—'I struck another match!' "

Jesus Christ waits for a crisis to come, for a crack to appear, or for your plans to be laid aside. Then He moves in and turns a tragedy into a triumph and a problem into your greatest opportunity!

> **I am looking for miracles—especially in the unexpected events of today!**

Welcome The Unexpected

*"I will praise the Lord no matter what happens. I will
constantly speak of his glories and grace."*

Psalm 34:1

How do you handle life's unwelcomed interruptions? We
all react differently. Think back over the events of the last
several weeks. Did anything happen unexpectedly?
Describe your unwelcomed interruption: _____

_____

_____

Describe your feelings and reactions: _____

_____

_____

_____

Describe how you wished you had reacted: _____

_____

_____

_____

Today, Lord, I am looking at every
interruption as a heaven-sent gift from
You. I can hardly wait!

Welcome The Unexpected

"God turned into good what was meant for evil."

Genesis 50:20

"Dr. Schuller, I believe in miracles!" said the man sitting next to me. Now when someone says those words to me, I'm ready to listen! "Tell me more," I enthused.

"Well," he continued, "I pride myself on getting to work on time. If the telephone rings when I am ready to leave the house, I tell my wife to tell them I have already left. And she always does, except for one morning.

"The phone rang and she said, 'He's just getting ready to leave.' I was muttering under my breath as I went and picked up the phone. Of all things, on the other end of the line was the one person I was trying to avoid. Now he had cornered me on the phone.

"Because of some business relationships, I could not simply cut him off, so I had to talk. I had to keep the other guy happy.

"Finally he was finished and I hung up, still muttering to my wife. At that point, my house shook and the ground seemed like water. It was the big quake of several years ago. I checked my watch and thought to myself, I would just now be at the bridge crossing the freeway. Later I would read in the paper that the bridge over which I was to have been at that moment had collapsed."

Don't resent those unwelcomed interruptions. God may be doing something beautiful through them!

> **God is bringing good
> out of every situation!**

Welcome The Unexpected

Thank you, Father, for the beautiful
surprises you are planning for me today.
So often in my life, when it looked like
the day would be
    dismal,
    depressing,
    dark,

an unexpected burst of
golden sunshine
exploded through a black cloud
sending inspiring shafts of warm,
beautiful sunshine into my life.

Father, it is happening now!
I can already feel the power of
your love, through Christ my Lord.

                Amen.

Welcome The Unexpected

"Who can ever list the glorious miracles of God? Who can ever praise him half enough?"

Psalm 106:2

One of the great missionaries of our day related to me the story of his conversion: While a student at Columbia University, he went through a long intellectual struggle, first as an agnostic, and then as an atheist.

Finally, while walking the streets of New York one night, he decided that if there is no God then nothing makes any sense. And he reached the point of utter and total despair.

Just then he was passing a church, and in a last desperate effort, he decided to go inside. He sat numb through the entire service, and when the minister called for a time of prayer at the end, he didn't close his eyes, he just looked around.

And then he spotted his physics professor sitting among the praying people. He was shocked! He thought, "My goodness, if my professor believes in God, maybe it's not such a crazy idea after all!" When the prayer time was over, he looked at the face of his professor and saw in that unguarded moment an aura and a spirit that was heavenly. It was, to him, proof of the existence of God.

At that moment he bowed his head and accepted Jesus Christ into his life. The whole direction of his life was changed as a result of an unexpected encounter!

I am giving in to the miracle of the unexpected. God is making my life more beautiful and complete through every experience!

Welcome The Unexpected

"O Lord, I will honor and praise your name, for you are my God; you do such wonderful things! You planned them long ago, and now you have accomplished them, just like you said!"

Isaiah 25:1

A few Sundays ago, when I was shaking hands after the service, I met a family from out of town. "Dr. Schuller," the mother said, "God has changed our lives!" Their little boy, who was not quite five years old, added, "Yes sir! We just found out about God!" About that time, the whole family was kind of misty-eyed.

I said to the little boy, "That's beautiful! Do you know what? God has a plan for you. I was about your age when I found out that God wanted me to be a preacher." And then I touched his little nose and repeated, "God has a plan for *you!*"

He looked up at me with his big eyes and said, "For me? For me?" "Yes," I replied, "for you." Then he looked up at his mother and said, "Mommy, for me!" And as he walked out the door I could still hear him saying to his mother, "For me!"

His whole life will be different because of that word and that touch. I know that for certain.

I invite you to be receptive. Today you will meet people you have never met before. You'll think it is a chance encounter. But God intends you to be a miracle in their life. In some way, because you meet, their life will never be the same. God will use you to make a miracle!

> God is in charge of every encounter in my life today. I am expecting miracles to happen because He is in charge!

Welcome The Unexpected

"No wonder we are happy in the Lord! For we are trusting him."

Psalm 33:21

Together the last few days, we have considered the ways God used the unexpected and even the unwelcome events in our lives for good. Today, I want to write the story. Describe some unexpected or unwelcome encounter you have experienced, and then write down how God used that event for something beautiful and good.

_____

_____

_____

_____

_____

_____

_____

_____

_____

_____

> **I am bold and courageous for I know that God is working everything out for good as I trust Him!**

Expect More

"My purpose is to give life in all its fullness."

John 10:10

W. Clement Stone said, "The greatest power available to man is the power of prayer." These are the words of an extremely successful business man. He has learned there can be no ultimate solutions to any of our problems unless we are in tune with God's spirit.

God is the source of all supply. It is god that makes the seed rupture and send its tender shoot through the spring soil, reaching to the sun. And the seed is not content until it produces and multiplies.

God is also the source of life and abundance in humans. Do you have a problem? Are you lacking anything? If you answer "yes" to these questions, then ask yourself, "Is the problem due to disharmony in my own life as it relates to people, to society and to God Himself?" If so, then you must get in tune with God's spirit through creative prayer.

Begin by praying, "Dear God, help me to see my blind spot. Open my eyes and my thinking to areas where I am not thinking correctly."

Then look at your problems with new vision, recognizing that all pain, all problems, including poverty, were really not designed by God to be the end of the road, but to be a bend in the road. The bend forces you to change direction—to change your thinking and do something differently.

> I see problems differently today.
> They are opportunities for new thinking
> and new directions!

Expect More

"The reason you don't have what you want is that you don't ask God for it."

James 4:2

If you have the feeling that there is a better life for you than what you have lived up to this point, then I believe that God Himself is trying to say something to you.

If you could have *anything* you asked for at this moment, what would you ask for? _____

_____

Write down two reasons why you do not presently have what you just wrote above: 1.) _____

_____

_____

2.) _____

_____

Now I want you to know that God believes in abundance and prosperity. Jesus said, "I am come that you might *have* . . ." He wants you to be among the haves, not among the have-nots! You can expect *more* out of life.

Become a possibility thinker today. Look at the two reasons you wrote above and add to the end of each sentence "BUT IT'S POSSIBLE!"

> **I believe that God is making it possible for me to enjoy a life of abundance today!**

Expect More

"And it is he who will supply all your needs from his riches in glory, because of what Christ Jesus has done for us."
                                                            Philippians 4:19

I know what problems are. I've had problems with people, I've had problems with myself, and I've had problems with God. But ultimately, I've found that all the problems were *my* problems. So now when I have a problem I begin by saying, "Oh God, what am I doing wrong?"

One problem I recall was my attitude toward selfishness. There was a time in my ministry when I felt that the job of a preacher was to condemn selfishness. But God revealed to me that selfishness is not to be condemned. It is to be pitied! Because every selfish person is immediately comdemning himself.

The selfish person is not enthusiastic. The selfish person is not happy. The selfish person is not prospering. These people do not have a lot of friends because other people seem to get their number and stay away from them.

The selfish husband loses his wife. The selfish boss loses employees and the selfish employee loses his job. Selfishness is its own condemnation and selfish people are to be pitied—then loved and redeemed through the changing power of Christ.

If you feel your desires are selfish, talk to God about your feelings. Remember, he wants you to prosper!

**I am giving lovingly to others and
I am richly blessed in return!**

Expect More

*"In everything you do, put God first, and he will direct you
and crown your efforts with success."*

Proverbs 3:6

When God gives you a dream of something more than
you presently enjoy, you can be sure of this: God's dream
will appear to be impossible! For when God thinks, He
always thinks bigger than you and I. And that's why God
wants you to use Possibility Thinking!

A few days ago, you wrote down a dream and then
described two reasons why your idea was impossible. Look
again at your dream and then consider this statement. "A
possibility thinker never brings the problem-solving phase
into the decision-making phase, or you are surrendering
leadership to problems instead of possibilities."

What I mean by that statement is that once you have the
dream, the next step is to make the right decisions, *without
considering the potential problems!* You simply *decide* to
commit yourself to your dream.

In looking at the dream God is giving you right now,
what decisions do you need to make immediately?

_____

_____

_____

_____

> **I have decided! Already I can feel God
> at work turning potential problems into
> exciting possibilities!**

Expect More

"In all that he does, he prospers."

Psalm 1:3 RSV

The car we were riding in was obviously a very expensive automobile. I commented to the driver, "It looks like you're doing very well." "Yes," he said, "by the grace of God, I am prospering."

He then told me his story. "Eleven years ago, at the age of 52, I didn't have a dime. I was broke but I had a dream. I wanted to run a restaurant and make a success out of it without getting involved in the liquor business. Everyone told me it couldn't be done.

"I read a book on ways to succeed through having the right attitude. The author said to never let a problem stop you. I needed money, so I went to a wealthy lumberman and presented my dream to him. Miraculously, he agreed to invest in my dream! Today I have six restaurants and my net worth is over a million dollars!

"But the exciting thing is what just happened recently. I have always been a tither. Last year, competing restaurants went up on both sides of my place. On top of that, the energy crisis forced us to eliminate our advertising lights. So my advertising source was cut and competitors were moving in. And then my pastor made an appeal to our church to double our tithe for the year. My wife and I prayed about it, doubled our tithe, and now here's the exciting news—last week my accountant said we doubled our business and doubled our net profits! God keeps working miracles!"

> **I am in tune with God's spirit. And He is the miracle worker!**

Expect More

"Your goodness and unfailing kindness shall be with me all of my life."

Psalm 23:6

What do I mean by prosperity? I do not mean a cold, calculating, unspiritual materialism. It is obvious that a person can become wealthy without the blessing of God. We often see people in the world who are enormously wealthy, but who have no joy. Real prosperity includes discovering deep joy in the whole process and feeling good while you move ahead.

W. Clement Stone, who is a friend of mine has said, "I've discovered that super rich people who do not really give generously, and who do not look upon their wealth as a stewardship from God, usually come to the end of their lives filled with bitterness, frequently committing suicide."

His statement reminds me of the Dead Sea. Fresh water comes from a brook and fills the Sea of Galilee, which is alive with fish. And then the Sea of Galilee takes that water and gives it to the Jordan River, which turns the desert into a rose and makes it the land of milk and honey. And finally, the Jordan River gives its water to the Dead Sea. The Dead Sea is dead because it does not give itself away!

This is a universal principle. If you want to live, you have to give. This is the key to prosperity. This is also the key to joyful living!

I give because I am rich knowing that I am in God's loving care!

Expect More

"A man will always reap just the kind of crop he sows."
                                        Galatians 6:7

What are you sowing? Seeds of generosity? Seeds of selfishness? Let's take a quick inventory.

In the past thirty days, I can recall sowing seeds of:

GENEROSITY	SELFISHNESS

Get in tune with God's spirit. Accept His loving forgiveness for your selfish actions, and thank Him for the opportunities for generosity.

**I am enriched by the power
of Christ within me!**

Expect Love

Lord, make me an instrument
   of Thy peace.
Where there is hatred, let me sow love;
Where there is injury, pardon;
Where there is doubt, faith;
Where there is despair, hope;
Where there is darkness, light;
Where there is sadness, joy;
O Divine Master, grant that I may
   not so much seek to be consoled, as
   console; to be understood, as to
   understand; to be loved, as to love.
For it is in giving, that we receive;
It is in pardoning, that we are pardoned;
It is in dying, that we are born to eternal life.

Amen

St. Francis of Assisi

Expect Love

"There is no fear in love."

1 John 4:18 RSV

I recall counseling with a lady whose marriage was ghastly. She was planning on a legal separation from her husband. We went through all kinds of counseling and seemed to make little progress. Finally one day I asked her, "Mary, why did you ever marry this guy in the first place?"

She started to tremble as she related her story to me. "When we first met he proposed marriage," she said. "But I didn't love him and said 'No.' His answer was, 'If you don't marry me, I'll kill myself.'

"I thought he was kidding. But he attempted suicide and ended up in the hospital. I felt guilty so I went to visit him. While there, he pleaded with me to marry him and this time I agreed."

And for 24 years she lived with him because she was *afraid* that if she left he would try to kill himself again. That's not love! That's *fear*. And fear produces horrible results. Love produces miraculous rewards!

A person becomes a beautiful Christian, not because he is against something or afraid of some horrible place, but because he is in love with someone named Jesus Christ. When you are in love with Him, your faith has a positive tap root and that makes all the difference in the world!

> **My roots are tapped into the positive stream of love—Jesus Christ. I am free to be a loving person!**

Expect Love

"And whatever you do, do it with kindness and love."
                              1 Corinthians 16:14

How would you define *love*? The emotion of love is so rich that it almost defies definition. I remember several years ago the "Happiness is . . ." fad. Everybody seemed to have a shirt, or at least a bumper sticker with their own example of happiness.

Let's try the same thing with *love*. St. Paul has given us a beginning point with our reading for today. Pick up where he left off and create your own descriptions of love.

Love is _____

Love is _____

Love is _____

Love is _____

Love is _____

Love is _____

Love is _____

Love is _____

Love is _____

Love is _____

> **I feel the power of God's love active within me, soothing, healing, and blessing me!**

Expect Love

Many waters cannot quench the flame of love, neither can the floods drown it."

Song of Solomon 8:7

I recently saw, on a friend's desk, a little prayer. It read, "Lord, today help me to make my words tender and sweet. Because tomorrow I'll have to eat them."

That thought reminded me of what a director of nurses told me. She expressed a very profound concept when she said, "When I train nurses, I say to them. 'Be a nutritious person; don't be a toxic person.'

"And then I explain what I mean. We have some nurses in our hospitals who are poorly trained. They are toxic people. Whenever they come into a room and either talk with a patient or touch them, they infect that person with the poison of fear, negativity, doubt and anxiety. Everything they do and say tears people down.

"We also have nurses who are nutritious persons," she continued. "The way they talk, the way they touch, the way they listen, the way they offer encouragement and the way they build hope, always puts nutritional strength into the patient. They create a mental attitude in which God can perform a healing ministry."

Are you a nutritious person? If you are dominated by love, you will be nutritious. You will be helpful to others, lifting them up with arms of love.

Love is lifting the weights off me and is giving me wings. I am free to love and be loved!

Expect Love

"God is love, and anyone who lives in love is living with God and God is living in him. And as we live with Christ, our love grows more perfect."

1 John 4:16, 17

We all know people who are nutritious, as my nursing friend described them. Who are the nutritious people in your life? List several of them:

_____

_____

_____

Why are these people nutritious? Describe some of their nutritious qualities: _____

_____

_____

_____

_____

Take the time today to either call or send a note of appreciation to one of your nutritious friends. Let them know how much they mean to you. That's being nutritious!

> Today is the day to speak of the love I have in my heart—for God, my family and my friends!

Expect Love

"Love each other with brotherly affection and take delight in honoring each other."

Romans 12:10

The last time I was in London I visited Harrod's Department store. I had heard so much about this unusual place that I decided I had to see for myself. When you enter the front door, there is a big sign which reads, "Enter into a new world." And believe me, that sign was true. You can purchase anything in that store, including a live elephant.

When I left Harrod's, I returned to my hotel and realized that I was supposed to make contact with the church office. I checked the phone directory to see how I could place a call from London to California. Then I noticed the hotel had instructions on the phone which read, "Now you can dial direct."

I was fascinated. I picked up the telephone, dialed the special number they told me to dial, added the church phone number and almost immediately heard, "Garden Grove Community Church, may I help you?"

Wow! What a world! Every day we should have a little sign in our mind that says, "Prepare to enter a new world!" Unfortunately, many people fear anything new. There is a normal inclination that we all have to flee to the shelter of the familiar. But when we experience love and are loving in return, we are captured by a confidence that gives us a spirit of adventure—love's reward!

> **The experience of love is helping me experience more of today!**

Expect Love

And I pray that Christ will be more and more at home in your hearts, living within you as you trust in him. May your roots go down deep into the soil of God's marvelous love; and may you be able to feel and understand, as all God's children should, how long, how wide, how deep, and how high his love really is; and to experience this love for yourselves, though it is so great that you will never see the end of it, or fully know or understand it.

Ephesians 3:17-19

Expect Growth

"But remember this—if you give little, you will get little. A farmer who plants just a few seeds will get only a small crop, but if he plants much he will reap much."

2 Corinthians 9:6

I believe in God! And I rejoice everytime I meet someone who has recently made the decision to become a beautiful believer, because God can now do something wonderful in their life.

There are infinite possibilities in little beginnings if God is present. I can understand this because of my experiences as a boy on our Iowa farm. Every year it seemed, we needed more food for the cattle and more grain to sell in the market. So my father would simply plow more ground and plant more seeds.

I learned a fundamental principle from those early experiences—if you need more, you have to give more! If you want a bigger harvest, you have to plant more seeds. For the laws of nature and growth are consistent: You reap according to what you sow.

My dad would look at a kernel of corn but he wouldn't see a kernel of corn. He would see a stalk breaking out of the ground and ears of corn growing out of the stalk. I think it was my father's example that inspired me to write, many years later: "Any fool can count the seeds in an apple, but only God can count the apples in a seed."

I am sowing more seeds of goodness and love. God is giving me an over-flowing harvest of goodness and love!

Expect Growth

"Keep on sowing your seed, for you never know which will grow—perhaps it all will."

Ecclesiastes 11:6

The miracle of the apple seed is an example of what god can do in any person's life. God wants you and me to enjoy a healthy, prosperous and abundant life.

God is constantly scattering seeds into your life. If you plant these seeds by faith, they will lead to new health, new strength, new abundance and prosperity. I see this principle everytime I read the book of Genesis. In the first ten chapters there is one verse repeated over and over again: "Be fruitful and multiply and replenish the earth." God has built into the system of nature enormous potential and possibility for growth. He wants to do the same with you!

What seeds are being planted within you by God today? Think about the possibilities for a moment and then write them down.

GOD'S SEEDS WITHIN ME

1. _____

2. _____

3. _____

4. _____

5. _____

> **My mind is open to the possibilities God has for me. I am cultivating the seeds He is planting!**

Expect Growth

"Plant the good seeds of righteousness and you will reap a crop of my love."

Hosea 10:12

We received a call at our Institute for Successful Church Leadership from a desperate pastor. He was ready to quit the ministry. He wanted to attend the institute, even though reservations were full.

We have a policy that people come first, so we allowed this man to come. The five days turned him around completely. He went back to his church enthused and excited about the ministry. In his suitcase was a stack of books he bought while here, including the book *Tara*—the story of the daughter of the producer of Hour of Power. Tara suffered a brain injury and is miraculously recovering.

Soon after this pastor returned to his hometown, a little girl was struck by a car and rushed to the hospital hovering on the brink of death. This pastor took a copy of the book, *Tara*, to the parents of this critically injured little girl and spent a great deal of time with them offering encouragement and faith.

The parents were non-church people. They read the book and it gave them great faith in God. They prayed and a miracle happened—their little girl recovered. Recently the entire family flew to California to worship with us. What a thrill it was to meet them. It all started with a little phone call!

Lord, I am paying attention to the little things You place in my life and I am expecting miracles to happen!

Expect Growth

*"If a man plants the good things of the Spirit, he will reap
the everlasting life which the Holy Spirit gives him."*
                                                    Galatians 6:8

How can you grow when there are so many distractions
around? Well, some people simply *mope* along, while
others *dope* their way through life. Some simply *grope*
their way, like a person walking through a dark maze. But
then there are the people who *hope* their way through.
They are the ones who have learned to look for the
possibilities in every situation.

I was riding down the freeway the other day and saw a
sign on the back of a truck, I've seen this sign in a variety
of places. It reads: *"Keep on Truckin'."*

Now I am not absolutely certain what that means, but I
do know that it is very popular! Then I got an idea. Why
not make a bumper sticker with three words that I
understand and firmly believe in, like *"Keep on
Possibilitizing!"*

Do you know what that means? I'll tell you.
Possibilitizing means imagining growth—visualizing what
it will look like in your life. It is praying for growth as you
begin to overcome, anticipate and overpower all the
obstacles which are placed in the path of growth and
victory.

And when you possibilitize, you multiply the potential
results. You multiply first in your mind all the great things
God *will* do and *can* do. And with all of these activities
going on in your mind, God is able to do even more than
you can imagine. Believe! It is possible!

> **My hope-building motto is: I will keep
> on possibilitizing all day!**

Expect Growth

"But thanks be to God, who gives us the victory through our Lord Jesus Christ."

1 Corinthians 15:57 RSV

Victory is yours! And when you are a Possibility Thinker, you keep your attention on the victory, not on the battle. You keep your eyes on the ultimate reward, not the pain. You see the crown instead of the cross.

Now that is not a denial of the reality of the pain, the cross, or the battle. But it is the perspective from which each of these is viewed. Without the reward in mind, the pain is unbearable. Without the crown, the cross is meaningless.

Are you fighting any battles today? Any pain in your life? Look at the reward and at the victory you will enjoy. How would you describe the victory or reward you are striving for?

_____

_____

_____

_____

_____

_____

Now that you can describe your victory, believe it!

**Through Christ, I am victorious!
Nothing will destroy the sense of joy
that comes with victory!**

Expect Growth

"They are like trees along a river bank bearing luscious fruit each season without fail. Their leaves shall never wither, and all they do shall prosper.

Psalm 1:3

Sometime ago I became very enthusiastic about olive trees. I was planting them on our church grounds at the time. Olive trees are found in Southern California, having been transplanted here from the Mediterranean region of the Middle East.

In my enthusiasm, I excitedly offered to send a young tree to anyone watching our Hour of Power program. We mailed out thousands of them and many of them arrived dried out. I received an interesting letter from a man who said, "I was so excited and happy when my package arrived. I gently opened the carton and to my surprise found a plastic bag with a tiny box and a dried out twig! What a letdown! I could have cried."

But he told me how he soaked the twig and placed it on a table where it received the sunlight. And soon the leaves had lifted and the tiny branch had turned itself to the sun. "I am excited again," he wrote, "and will let you know how it grows."

As I read his letter, I wondered how many olive trees were thrown away because people did not have the faith to believe they would live. Who can count the olives in a twig that looks so lifeless? Use the faith God gives you to believe and grow!

> The stream of life that comes from God is flowing through me giving life to dreams and ideas!

Expect Growth

At the beginning of a new day,
Lord,
I sit in a choice seat.
I wait expectantly
for the curtain to go up
and
for the drama to begin.

Lord, at the end of this day,
I will have been deeply changed,
for I will have grown
as I open myself more and more
to the reality of the love of God
at work within me!

Thank you Lord!

Expect Miracles!

"So whoever has God's Son has life."

1 John 5:12

I was speaking at one of the seminaries in the East and had the opportunity to meet and talk with a number of well-known theologians and professors during my visit.

But one man stood out from all the others I met. I was on my way to the library to find a quiet corner where I could study, prepare and meditate. This young man spotted me as I entered the library. He ran up to me and exclaimed, "Dr. Schuller!" As we shook hands, he continued, "I was converted in your church six years ago." And his face beamed as he described the event.

I shared his enthusiasm, even though I had to admit to him that I did not remember him. He said, "That's okay, I knew you wouldn't remember me. I've been away at a Christian college four years and here at seminary for almost a year. The important thing is that your ministry introduced me to my Savior, Jesus Christ." We must have talked almost an hour together and what a rich experience that was.

He was converted in my church and was now preparing to be a minister himself, and I never knew it until we met at seminary! And that was the highlight of my visit, because he reminded me again that we have an influence that provides a channel for God to work miracles. And a hundred million miracles are happening every day, but only those who have the faith will spot them on life's way.

> **My heart is tuned to the miracle-working God!**

Expect Miracles!

For unto us a Child is born; unto us a Son is given.
                                                    Isaiah 9:6

There were still seven shopping days left before Christmas. As I passed my youngest daughter, Gretchen's room, I noticed she was sitting on the floor surrounded with envelopes and sheets of clean stationery. On closer inspection, it looked like she was busy writing letters. Now Gretchen *never* writes letters, so naturally my curiosity was aroused.

"Gretchen," I exclaimed, "what are you doing?" Caught by surprise, she looked up at me with a big smile and said, "Oh, hi dad. I'm writing my thank you notes."

"You're what?" I asked.

"I am starting to write my thank you notes for Christmas now, so you and mom won't have to bother me about it after Christmas," she explained.

A little confused at this point, I continued, "Gretchen, how can you write thank you notes for presents you haven't received? How do you know who to address them to or what you'll be receiving?"

"Oh," she enthused, "I've got that all figured out. I'm going to say, 'Dear Friend, thank you for your wonderful gift. I'm enjoying it very much. Love, Gretchen.'"

I laughed at her ingenuity and said, "But, Gretchen how do you know you will enjoy all the gifts?" "Oh," she countered, "I just know I'm going to."

That's what you call advance planning. But her anticipation produced within her a spirit of joyful expectancy. She was living in the arena of goodness. When you expect things to happen to you, your attitude will change, your spirits will soar, your face will beam and you will be filled with joy and enthusiasm for the day.

**Thank you, God,
for Your wonderful gift!**

Expect Miracles!

"When someone becomes a Christian he becomes a brand new person inside. He is not the same any more. A new life has begun!"

2 Corinthians 5:17

The miracle of conversion is probably the greatest miracle of all. Don't let the word "conversion" frighten you. That word means you can be born out of dullness into vitality, out of death into life, out of drabness into enthusiasm, out of fear into courage, out of doubt into faith, out of hostility into love—because of Jesus Christ!

Have you been converted? Have you experienced the miracle of new life? If so, recall the event and describe what happened:

_____

_____

_____

_____

_____

_____

If not, read John 3 and then ask Jesus Christ to come into your life and make you a new person!

> **I am continuously being changed through the power of Christ. I am becoming brand new!**

Expect Miracles!

"Hallelujah! I want to express publicly before his people my heartfelt thanks to God for his mighty miracles."

Psalm 111:1

Mrs. Schuller and I were on a cruise to Norway and Sweden. We were at sea for several days and still had not had the opportunity to meet the Captain. But as we were walking on the deck we suddenly stopped in our tracks when the intercom came on and we heard, "This is your Captain speaking."

Everyone else stopped when they heard this voice with his beautiful Scandinavian accent. As we listened, we did not know what he looked like, but we did know it was his voice.

All of us ride on a ship called Planet Earth. We are spinning at an incredible rate, flying through the universe. And I have news for you—there is a Captain, even though you haven't seen Him.

Believe in Him and sometime, somehow, someway He will speak to you through an event, an emotion, the Bible or a friend. You will hear the announcement, "This is your Captain speaking." At that moment of faith, miracles begin. For miracles cannot occur without faith. And faith only happens when you begin to cast yourself out on a great idea that is seemingly impossible. And the concept of God as the Captain of your soul is the beginning point!

God is my captain. I am trusting Him for today and tomorrow!

Expect Miracles!

"My help is from Jehovah who made the mountains! And the heavens, too!"

Psalm 121:1

One way to describe the miraculous relationship you and I have with God is the idea of the relationship a captain has with his ship. David refers to his relationship with God in the image of the shepherd. When you think of the relationship you have with God, what other ideas, symbols or images can you think of to describe that relationship?

The Lord is my _____

_____

_____

_____

_____

_____

_____

The most accurate image any of us have of God is the person of Jesus Christ. Jesus is the heartbeat of God to the world. And He loves YOU and ME!

> **Think of it! The God of the universe loves me! How can I ever be afraid or perplexed?**

Expect Miracles!

"Praise him for his mighty works. Praise his unequaled greatness."

Psalm 150:2

Early one morning during a session of our Institute for Successful Church Leadership, a minister from Minnesota was suddenly called out for an emergency call. He was told that his three-and-a-half year old son had fallen into a swimming pool. His wife had lifted the little boy out of the pool and applied artificial respiration to his lifeless body. When the ambulance arrived, the boy was beginning to respond.

The whole congregation of 400 ministers joined with me in praying for that little baby. And what a great moment it was at the closing of the convocation, during the dedication service, to see the little lad and his parents come forward to kneel at the front of the church. I don't believe there was a dry eye anywhere.

After that service, the father told me that when they arrived at the hospital, x-rays showed that there was water in his son's lungs. Several hours after we had all joined in prayer, they x-rayed his lungs again and found no water present!

The doctor said, "It's a miracle!" And it was! For it only takes you and God to make a miracle!

> Thank you, God, for the mountains in my life that You and I are turning into miracles!

Expect Miracles!

"Bring all the tithes into the storehouse so that there will be food enough in my Temple; if you do, I will open up the windows of heaven for you and pour out a blessing so great you won't have room enough to take it in!"

Malachi 3:10

I saw a bumper sticker the other day that read, "If you love the Lord, don't honk—tithe! If you don't know what that word means, it simply is the action of giving God one tenth of the money you earn.

Now tithing illustrates God's ability to work miracles! There are many people who never have miracles happen in their lives because they never take a chance. I know many people, though, who have many miracles take place in their lives after they start tithing.

The money they earn may not be enough to stretch out and pay their bills. But they believe God, when in the Bible He says, if you give a tenth of what you earn to Him, He will perform miracles.

I recall while in seminary struggling with this. But whenever I earned a little money, I took a tenth of it and put it in the offering plate. It has been an amazing thing—for over 30 years, God continually surprises me with his miracle-working ways. I started the miracle. But only God can finish the miracle!

What is God waiting for you to do before he can finish his miracle-working activity? _____

_____

I commit myself to begin God's miracle working activity today!

Expect Miracles!

"Jesus' disciples saw him do many other miracles . . . but these are recorded so that you will believe that he is the Messiah, the Son of God, and that believing in him you will have life."

John 20:30-31

Pat Shaughnessy was one of the people severely injured in a bomb explosion in Los Angeles airport. He is a minister in Arizona, and was on his way to spend a month preaching throughout South Korea. When the bomb went off, three people standing around him were killed. He found himself lying on the floor with his knee blown apart. He received eleven units of blood in the hospital and lost his right leg.

He told me, "They said I'd be in intensive care for one or two weeks. I was there for one and a half days. And God has used this experience in a miraculous way. He knew the bomb was there, and He knew I was there. It was not an *accident*, it was an *incident* in the life of a Christian.

"And through this incident God has expanded our ministry in a wonderful way. I was not the victim of that bomb blast, I was the victor. You see, my reaction to life is based on what I believe. And I believe that Jesus Christ allows everything to happen in our lives for a purpose.

"So many people ask me, 'What happened to your leg?' 'Oh, I was in a bombing.' I tell them. When they say, 'That's too bad' I respond by saying, 'No, it's not. Let me tell you what happened. Let me tell you about Jesus Christ.' " Pat turned a tragedy into a miracle, because he knows personally the miracle-working God!

Every incident in my life today is an opportunity for God to work a miracle!